RE-SOUNDING

introducing an alternative metaphor for organization change

Rik Spann & Simon Martin

RE-SOUNDING

First published as an eBook by Taos Institute Publications in 2021

First Printing this edition, 2021

Cover design based on the Real Book series of hand-produced music lead sheets used by some jazz musicians.

In all cases, the editors and writers have made efforts to ensure that the text credits are given to appropriate people and organizations. If any infringement has been made, we will be glad, upon receiving notification, to make appropriate acknowledgement in future editions of the book.

ISBN: 978-1-5272-9171-3

I am very pleased to see the wonderful work that Rik Spann and Simon Martin are doing. Their light-hearted and musical approach is grounded in real depth of thought and scholarship. Organizations of all kinds are ready for a change, toward a more adaptive way of being that takes account of the complexity of the contemporary world and of human inter-action. Every industry needs this kind of adaptation, to recog-nize itself as part of ever-changing nature and culture. To be flexible is to endure and grow.

Stephen Nachmanovitch,
author of *The Art of Is* and *Free Play*

For
Noah
Abel
Marleen

For
Niamh
Áine
Ruairí

CONTENTS

CONTENTS

Sound Track

We've put together some recommended listening for each of the sections of this book. It's an invitation, not a requirement! You might like to listen to these tracks before you read each section, or maybe while you read. It's up to you.

To get started:
Générique (L'Ascenseur pour l'Échafaud), Miles Davis

Chapter One:
Cool Struttin', Sonny Clark

Chapter Two:
The Sidewinder, Lee Morgan

Chapter Three:
Kind of Blue, Miles Davis

Chapter Four:
Stolen Moments, Oliver Nelson

New places to stand

*To see a World in a Grain of Sand
And a Heaven in a Wild Flower,
Hold Infinity in the palm of your hand
And Eternity in an hour.*

William Blake

You might like to read this while listening to:

Cool Struttin', Sonny Clark

In many ways a lot of the challenges we face today can be seen as problems of perspective. We seem to have become hard-wired to operate from particular positions, and even as these approaches show diminishing returns (or even significant losses) we try even harder to make the same approaches work. This is no new folly. As Einstein put it, "we cannot solve our problems with the same level of thinking that created them" (Rowe & Schulman, 2007, p. 383). But we try nonetheless. And at times of particular challenge it seems we struggle more with finding new perspectives. As we write, Coronavirus is spreading around the globe. It is noticeable in the language of many leaders around the world that we are "at war" with the virus, pitting ourselves against an "enemy", "hitting it with force". It doesn't quite seem to cut it, seems hollow somehow – "…sound and fury / Signifying nothing…" (Shakespeare, 1962, p. 193 (originally 1606)). In their research into "leadership in a permanent crisis" Heifetz and Linsky (2009) talk about the difficulty we have as leaders in differentiating between situations that are "technical problems" and those that are "adaptive challenges".

Technical problems may be complicated, but with enough effort, and expertise drawn from our experiences of the past, they are solvable. They may require tweaks and incremental improvements to approaches, but they exist within a version of the status quo.

Adaptive challenges are complex. They require changes across many boundaries, with many variables, and cannot be analysed or parsed into their constituent parts in order to be 100% sure of the right path of action. They require experimentation, changes in perspective, and maybe even changes in beliefs and values.

Our "hard-wiring", particularly at times of anxiety and duress, is often to reach for the known and operate from the technical perspective. However, if it is a true adaptive challenge we are facing, our success will be short-lived. An example Heifetz and Linsky give is that of a patient who has suffered a heart attack. Technical expertise may help save them in the short term. But if the adaptive challenge of lifestyle changes (which probably link to these beliefs, habits, values, perspectives) is not risen to, then the prognosis is unlikely to be good longer term.

We seem highly susceptible to the allure of one truth, and often an old truth at that; and struggle to examine the origins of these truths and the assumptions that underpin them. Gareth Morgan's work looks at how the dominant perspective(s) we hold on organization (and by extension, society) shape what we do:

"...all theories of organization and management are based on implicit images or metaphors that lead us to see, understand, and manage organizations in distinctive yet partial ways."

(Morgan, 1997, p. 4)

He notices that the dominant perspective that still shapes our approaches is the idea of the organization as a machine. He traces its roots back further to the practice of military organizing, where dividing duty and responsibility into hierarchy and rank meant you could break down and apportion tasks in a contained and controlled way. And then sees it journey through the Industrial Revolution, where ideas of production line construction saw craft processes broken into stages, driving efficiencies of speed and cost. And he highlights that any dominant perspective emphasizes some things, but disappears others. For example, the machine metaphor might deemphasize the significance of serendipity, experimentation, the "happy accident"; or draw a veil over the existence of shadow organizations, political power structures that operate beyond the "clear division" of rank and hierarchy. He then goes on to explore alternative perspectives on organizing, such as organizations as "neural networks", or "cultures", or "psychic prisons". Looking from these new perspectives can open up other ways of understanding a situation, and provide different options for action as leaders and participants in organization.

And this ability to entertain multiple perspectives is something Morgan sees as a key skill:

"Skilled leaders and managers ... have a capacity to remain open and flexible, suspending immediate judgements...They are aware that new insights often arise as one approaches situations from "new angles"...Less effective managers and problem solvers, however, seem to interpret everything from a fixed standpoint."

(Morgan, 1997, pp. 3-4)

We are aware that this is not necessarily new thinking, however, it is still far from the mainstream. Finding ways to move away from the draw of fixity of standpoint, the draw of one truth, one narrative still seems important work which will require constant, deliberate practice.

And another key influence in our thinking about ways of reaching for new insight and new perspectives is Heron and Reason's work into an extended epistemology (2008, p. 367). If we take epistemology to be the theory of how we know things, then Heron and Reason's work suggests that there might be more routes to knowledge than we currently (frequently or deliberately) use. They talk about there being 4 "ways of knowing":

- Propositional
- Practical
- Experiential
- Presentational

Propositional and **Practical** ways of knowing are far more established in modern organizational life. These are ways of knowing founded in policy, process, best practice procedures gleaned from the experience of what has happened in the past, and what "normally works" (propositional); or skills and competencies developed through repeatedly carrying out these processes and operational procedures (practical). **Experiential** knowing is described as the embodied encounter with the experience of the moment; the second by second unfolding of everything that happens. And **Presentational** knowing is the intuitive processing of this experience into "artistic form". Rather than drawing primarily on past experience to establish norms, these two ways of knowing focus on data from the (recent) present, and on working with these data to "create" new perspectives.

When we are dealing with simple organizational situations, then Propositional and Practical knowing may serve us well (for example Heifetz and Linsky's "technical problem", or Morgan's "machine" organization). However, when dealing with complex systemic questions, or "adaptive challenges" such as organizational or societal change, we would do well to explore the other forms of knowing too. And this is what we are hoping to draw on in this book. It is not a new struggle. A whole body of social constructionist thinking (Gergen, 2009) has shown that our reality(ies) are co-created in the tasks and attitudes that we adopt together in our families, organizations, societies, cultures. And yet at the same time we notice we, as a society, are still trying to codify propositions that pin the butterfly of truth to the mounting card of a constant world. And this is not where we have been for some time, or perhaps ever were. So that's what this is about, trying to find **new places to stand** to try and see and hear what is going on, what we are doing.

And at times it can be overwhelming, and any experiments seem frivolous, or too small to make a difference. Yet behind these efforts, in our stronger moments, is a theory of change which draws courage from Gestalt thinker Arnold Beisser:

"Change does not take place through a coercive attempt by the individual or by another person to change...but it does take place if one takes the time and effort...to be fully invested in his current positions."

(Beisser, 1970)

This exploration is about trying to find new ways to see and hear what it is we are doing, and what options might open up if we can move away from the fixity of some of our dominant perspectives.

Really noticing what we are doing is hard enough; but might be enough.

Oxford & Amsterdam, March, 2020

2

The road to here

...he only takes portions of existence and fancies it the whole...

William Blake

You might like to read this while listening to:

The Sidewinder, Lee Morgan

Our conversations in and around our work have ranged widely. We are fond of digression, and unexpected directions. And at the same time appreciate that this type of thinking is not always easy to follow and share. However, in the process of shaping and working with alternative perspectives on organizations, we are of course also drawing on a tradition of organizational thinking, some of which it is worth tracing here.

Ways of thinking about organization
The knowledge we inherit about organizations is still heav-

ily influenced by traditional sciences. Complexity thinker Ralph Stacey sees these as a "project to get closer and closer to certainty" (Stacey, 2003, p. 28), and indeed, this lens on the world has led to a great many beneficial insights and developments. However, the "success" of traditional science has led to it shaping the dominant discourse around how things work, and often we are applying these assumptions unquestioningly to all situations and contexts we find ourselves in, with a risk of oversimplification.

In many cases, what unfolds is something far messier, and whilst we are busy planning, there is probably a whole lot happening that we are missing out on. Again, to give the word to Stacey:

"Instead of asking the question, what should we do, I always ask the question, what are we doing?"

(Stacey, 2003, p. 32)

Stacey views organizations as "complex responsive processes" whereby we each bring our own intentions, hopes and hang-ups and express them through gestures which others respond to in their own unique and unpredictable ways (building on George Herbert Mead and Norbert Elias's work on social process and attitudes). It is this gesturing and responding to each other which is the basis for organizational action. Add into this mix the idea of power dynamics and our ability to enable and constrain each other in a wide and creative variety of ways, and we perhaps have something close to the messiness of organizational life we often experience.

With so much going on in the here and now, if we are interested in working well in, and even changing, organizations, we must focus first and foremost on what it is we *are* doing. Otto Scharmer talks about the job of organizational consulting being to "make it possible for the [organizational] system to sense and see itself" (Scharmer, 2018, p. xiii). He shares Stacey's view that energy and choices for change are likely to come from paying close attention to what it *is* we are currently doing together, as it raises natural questions around what is helpful, and what isn't. Scharmer's metaphor is a visual one, the idea, perhaps, of "holding up a mirror" to an organization. It speaks to the watchable theatre of everyday organizational life, and indeed Scharmer works very richly with theatrical techniques. Anthropological approaches to working with culture and organization draw on the visual metaphor too. American anthropologist Clifford Geertz talks about creating "thick descriptions" of cultures and social organizations through nuanced and layered observation and vivid depiction of the current state, rather than jumping straight to "objective" analysis (Geertz, 1973, p. 6). And visual metaphor abounds in organizational life too, as leaders set out their "visions" for the future and take aim at various "targets" in the distance. It can be a powerful and helpful metaphor. And whilst we may try to heed the words of American scientist and philosopher Alfred Korzybski and remember that "the map is not the territory" (Korzybski, 1994, p.

58) we notice that this metaphor is often unconsciously dominant in organizational languages.

And as Morgan noticed the dominance of the machine metaphor in organizational life, and wondered what it might be overshadowing or disappearing, we became interested in turning to some of the other senses and thinking also about ***sound – how we listen, hear and speak into organizations***. We are communicating all the time in organizational life, and a lot of our most intentional acts as leaders are verbal and voiced, in the formal and informal conversations we have all day every day. Organizational consultant and complexity thinker, Patricia Shaw, goes as far as saying that:

"Organizing is conversational process and organizational change is shifts in the patterning of conversation"

(Shaw, 2002, p. 124)

Organizations are the composite of what we are currently saying and not saying to each other, hearing and not hearing; the patterned sound we make together. Moving to an alternate organization state, therefore, is about noticing what we are saying and not saying to each other, hearing and not hearing, and disrupting these patterns. We cannot be sure of the impact of any changes we make, as the ways people respond to what we do differently will be deeply their own. Change becomes an "ensemble improvisation" (Shaw, 2002, p. 96). It requires a playfulness, an attentiveness; and above all an attentiveness to the "audible". How are we speaking and responding to one another?

Music as metaphor

Given this perspective we have found music (patterned sound organized in time) a rich metaphor for thinking about how we live, and lead in the organizations in which we participate (and we have noticed at times how hard it can be to stay with it – the lure of the visual metaphor is everywhere, as we find ourselves talking about tonal *palettes*, *blue* notes, *dark* harmonies...). And when we think about organizational sound and music, we are not really thinking of the somewhat heroic image of leader as conductor of an orchestra (in many ways this metaphor, with its individualistic leader and the idea of each instrument knowing its part, can be seen as a recasting of the idea of the organization as a planned mechanism). Rather we have found resonance with our organizational experiences in the messier lives and practices of gigging rock and jazz musicians, negotiating their art alongside other demands and challenges, and producing some of the classic pieces of music we enjoy today. For example, Keith Richards abandoning standard guitar tuning for banjo tuning at a time when the Rolling Stones were struggling to innovate their song writing. Letting go of the standard way of doing things opened him up to find the riffs that formed some of their best-known hits. Or a relatively unknown Tracy Chapman standing in for Stevie Wonder at a packed Wembley in 1988 at a moment's notice. Overcoming her anxiety, stepping into the newness of the situation rather than seeking safety, led to one of her most memorable performances and kick-started her career. Or Miles Davis arriving at a New York recording studio for the seminal *Kind of Blue* sessions with scraps of paper in his hands; modal scales which set the frame within which the players were to improvise. Rather than trying to plan for every eventuality, convening the right people and giving them just enough structure to start, led to one of the most influential recordings ever made, whose impact on music (and on us as we'll see in the next chapter) is still being felt today.

3

The Batesonian instinct

Never vote for a man who is neither a poet or an artist or a birdwatcher...

Gregory Bateson

You might like to read this while listening to:

Kind of Blue, Miles Davis

Having traced how our thinking has developed out of the influences and works of others, we're aware we have emphasized a process that seems linear and incremental. However, we feel it's important also to acknowledge the influence of serendipity, whim, instinct, playfulness, call it what you will. We first met at a workshop on improvisation in a yoga studio on the banks of the river Spree on three hot summer's days in Berlin. The workshop was being run by musician, improviser, and educator Stephen Nachmanovitch (Stephen was also a student under the great thinker across disciplines, Gregory Bateson, in the later stages of his career at the University of California; and Bateson seems to be a presiding influence behind our work to this day). Neither of us knew what to expect from the workshop; and both of us had acted out of the instinct that trying something new and unknown was likely to lead to learning, news of difference, with a good chance of fun. We were told to bring what musical instruments we had, but that we could not play them in normal ways. We arrived, took our shoes off, and the rest stays with those who were there.

What this "meeting" represents for us is yet another experience in our lives that affirms the value of different approaches, different combinations, cross-pollinating arts, sciences, social sciences. It is exciting and revealing when you start considering things, which society (or the "academy") says don't belong together, alongside one another; and being curious as to what there might be to be learned. It is what we have come, in our conversations, to describe as a "Batesonian instinct". Bateson's work was characterized by his urge to draw on knowledge from diverse fields; so much so that for much of his academic career he was almost departmentally homeless. He made advances in fields as varied as anthropology, biology, cybernetics, family therapy, ecology and aesthetics to mention but some. Yet whilst academic departments were either keen to claim him, or reject him, depending on where they were standing, his driving interest remained the desire to find "the pattern which connects" (Bateson, 2002, p. 7). Alfonso Montuori talks about this instinct being a "transdisciplinary" approach rather than "multidisciplinary" (Montuori, 2005, p. 147). The distinction for him is that Bateson was interested in what might be learnt at the meta level, rather than simply deepening knowledge of different disciplines.

It is this instinct that we have been trying to follow in our work. If we are curious about considering what is going on in organizations from different angles, through the lenses of different fields and bodies of knowledge, what surprises might result?

Liner notes...

Some time ago we began capturing reflections from regular discussions about possible connections between Miles Davis's seminal album *Kind of Blue*, and Bateson's work (particularly *Steps to an Ecology of Mind*). The idea here was to hold these two bodies of work together with some of the charge of metaphor, where energy and new perspectives are generated by connecting words and phrases that "don't normally belong together". Bateson himself was fond of a similar approach to making unusual, interesting and useful connections, a basic intellectual strategy which Mary Catherine Bateson termed "the search for insight through analogy" (Bateson & Bateson, 2004, p. 64).

Similarly, the original liner notes to *Kind of Blue* use analogy to talk about how Davis and the band viewed their work. Pianist, Bill Evans, writes of the Japanese art of calligraphy, where producing work with one stroke of the brush is the pinnacle of years of artistic training – in this case an analogue for the improvised works of collective genius captured (for the most part in one take) in two short studio sessions in March and April 1959.

So, buoyed by the permission to work metaphorically by yoking ideas from different categories together, this was both our method and our madness here, as we considered Bateson's work alongside the 5 tracks of *Kind of Blue*. The following are resonances and echoes that resulted from the practice of holding these thinkers / performers / actors next to each other in the crucible of our conversations.

For those of you unfamiliar with *Kind of Blue* you might also like to try listening to one or two tracks whilst lightly holding an organizational question or challenge you have in mind. We tend to let our minds go fuzzy and try to be curious about the associations that crop up. Without any pressure on them being useful, in time we usually realize that they are.

No. 1 "So What" – the art of convening

"So What" was recorded second but selected to be the first track on the album. When we listen and reflect on it, it speaks to us most about the art of convening and setting a frame. Davis was responsible for booking the sessions and getting the musicians in the room, in this case a deconsecrated Armenian Orthodox church in New York City. And the improvisational frame he set them was a series of modal scales, in the case of "So What" based on the Dorian mode (the white keys on a piano from D to D with a bluesy flattened 3rd and 7th). This provided them with enough structure to work with, and outlined the territory which they were going to explore together.

But providing a loose structure around which to collectively improvise is nothing new in jazz at this stage. For us the key shift is in the harmonic drive. Traditional "hot jazz" to this point was built on a series of chord progressions and a driving beat which was all about agency and moving through tension to resolution. With the modal scalar structure this drive is emphasized less. The musicians stay in one tonal space for much longer, and the harmonic progression is much slower. We listen and hear differently, as did the musicians in the studio on that day.

Richard Williams, in his great associative book on *Kind of Blue* and its influences, talks about how Davis allowed the piano, drums and bass to "participate in the dialogue", bringing the rhythm section into the conversation (*The Blue Moment*, Williams, 2009, p. 19). And it is this analogy with types of conversations that we're drawn to as we make associations with this piece. The modal frame in "So What" gives it the quality of a true, deep, reflective dialogue. The participants in the conversation are clear enough about what they are talking about and the language they are using (everything within the Dorian mode). They stay with the subject and don't rush onto other agenda items (the harmonic development is slow and they are not rushing through chord changes to the resolution). For the time they are together they are present and open to what they might discover.

And this is the type of dialogue Bateson was also keen to facilitate in his work. Stephen Nachmanovitch, as a former student of his, talks about how he liked "to get a nice juicy silence" going within conversations he convened, creating the conditions for deep reflection, listening and learning (Nachmanovitch, 1981, p. 3). A place to dwell and explore without the pressure of agency. How often in our organizational lives are we rushing through the chord changes of another jazz "standard" when with the right people, place and frame we could be finding out something new?

Unheroic as it may seem (and is!), convening and holding spaces where people can create and explore ideas without rushing to the obvious conclusion is a much-needed leadership act.

N.B. we have subsequently realized that the final chapter in Bateson's *Mind and Nature: A Necessary Unity* is titled "So What?" (Bateson, 1979, p. 203). We can neither confirm or deny a link but enjoy the speculation...

No. 2 "Freddie Freeloader" – hanging out with the unusual suspects

The first track recorded, but second on the album, "Freddie Freeloader", is named for a larger-than-life Philadelphia character who hung out with the band when they were in town, and who, by all accounts, was shy about standing a round of drinks! Nevertheless, there is an accepting appreciation in naming the track for him. And this speaks to us about the value of hanging out with the unusual suspects. If, in the conversations we convene, we can include people with different backgrounds, life experiences, and perspectives to us, then we are more likely to learn something new and not just have our own comfortable truths confirmed to us.

One of Bateson's maxims was "never vote for a man who is neither a poet or an artist or a birdwatcher" (Charlton, 2008, p. 100). And in this we hear an argument against two-dimensional specialism or "professionalism". Given the complex connected world we live in, narrow perspectives are of limited use in trying to get a sense of the whole. If we have chemists who can only think like chemists, accountants who can only think like accountants, and politicians who can only think like politicians, then the choices we have in front of us are likely to be less creative. And we need to create an environment where people sharing their difference is accepted and positively encouraged. Let the Head of Operations share her inner birdwatcher and not hide behind a mask of "gravitas", let the uncertain watercolourist peep out from behind the desk of the risk specialist.

In fact this transdisciplinary urge defines Bateson's work, spanning, as it does, so many different fields. This was not always easy for him, as academic institutions were keen to label him as one thing or another. At the heart of this though was his keen sense that the peripheries and intersections of various disciplines were where the learning needed would come from. And indeed, in complex systems, change often (or almost always) starts with a disturbance or difference at the periphery. So, if change and innovation (newness) are what we need in our organizations, who are the poets and birdwatchers, the unusual suspects we should be hanging out with and inviting into our meetings and conversations? Let the finger-snapping coolness of "Freddie Freeloader" stand as an anthem for the different characters and perspectives we need in our lives.

Actively seeking out and inviting different people and perspectives (especially those that seem unlikely) into our conversations can open up new possibilities and be a check against our own delusions.

No. 3 "Blue in Green" – helping the system see and hear itself

One of the things that strikes us about "Blue in Green" is its unusual 10 bar structure. The normal pattern in jazz standards would be combinations of 8 and 16 bar sections, or 12 bars for a blues structure. What this 10 bar variation seems to us to do, is draw attention to the form of the track so that we experience it more consciously. We are so used to the standard patterns that we can listen to music in this form and it slides off our consciousness. It becomes background music which careers to its obvious cadential conclusion. "Blue in Green" would seem to have different designs on our attention.

Bateson talks about working from a systemic perspective being a job of "finding the pattern that connects". It requires an open and present attentiveness to what is going on in the here and now in a system, which is very different to the half-consciousness of humming along to "Hello Dolly". If we listen and look intently enough we may be able to discern an underlying and unifying "rightness" or aesthetic sense to whatever it is we are examining. And in some ways that's the muscle that the 10 bar structure in "Blue in Green" is training. Through the creative constraint set by the form, the musicians are being forced to explore the essence of a 12 bar blues and recast it in 10 bars. They are forced to pay attention in a way that romping through the familiar chord sequence of a 12 bar blues does not require. And there is something slightly off-kilter about the structure that keeps us, as listeners, attentive too. We sense the exquisite tension and strain as our inner ear tries to anticipate a 12 bar pattern and is denied it. We are learning about this 10 bar form. And somehow by comparison we are being allowed to see and hear the 12 bar form afresh too.

This experience speaks to us of ways of viewing change in organizational systems. As mentioned above, management thinker Otto Scharmer speaks of organizational change work being about "helping the system sense and see itself" (Scharmer, 2018, p. xiii). When we are nested within our organizational systems and cultures it can be very hard for us to notice what it is we are all doing together, and ask whether it is helpful. Our normal modus operandi is humming along to a familiar 12 bar blues structure with our attention elsewhere. Scharmer's "theory of change" suggests that it is important to find ways of holding a mirror up to the existing organizational and cultural patterns, dynamics, behaviours, routines and rituals. Without necessarily planning the future state, "paying attention to what is", to bring back again the words of Gestaltist Arnold Beisser, can often generate enough energy and choice for change (Beisser, 1970). If we can see what it is we are doing then we can ask if it is helpful. Moving to the auditory metaphor, what we are experiencing in "Blue in Green" is a model in miniature of a system (in this case the 12 bar blues) "sensing and *hearing* itself" afresh.

Finding ways of seeing and hearing our organizational patterns and cultures afresh is a key step towards releasing energy and options for change.

No. 4 "All Blues" – self-regulation and (social) change

"All Blues" is characterized by its see-sawing 6/8 time riff and rhythm climbing relentlessly up and down over a minor third. When we listen to this there is a tightness to it; a sense of pressure sealed within the container of the frame that

Davis has set for the band. There is a tension and darkness that is being explored and worked out, which never quite bubbles over but manages to check itself.

For us, this has associations with Bateson's work in the area of cybernetics and looking at how systems regulate themselves. As so often with Bateson, the seeds of this thinking are found at the periphery or boundary of another body of knowledge, in this case his early anthropological work in the 1930's with the Iatmul tribe in New Guinea. In studying the tribe's social interactions Bateson noticed that group dynamics progressed through a mix of complementary and symmetrical patterns of behaviour, which he referred to as schismogenesis. Symmetrical patterns of behaviour match each other and lead to escalation, for example, if the appropriate cultural response to aggression is more aggression, then the situation will eventually get very heated. Complementary patterns reinforce each other, for example, if the appropriate cultural response to dominance is submission then increased dominant interactions from some parties will call forth increased submission in others. Bateson noticed that both patterns had the potential to become extreme and lead to social break up. What stopped this happening was the *Naven* ritual, where family groups in tension come together regularly to celebrate cultural milestones, and relieve the pressure built up through the pattern of their social interactions.

These ideas re-emerge in Bateson's later work in the concept of positive (symmetrical) and negative (complementary) feedback loops in cybernetic systems. And a particularly potent example of symmetrical schismogenesis was soon to be supplied on the geopolitical stage, through the Cold War arms race between the US and the Soviet Union. And perhaps that's also what we hear bubbling and cooking in this track, recorded right in the middle of the Cold War: the complex escalations and de-escalations of a political world working out if it's going to overheat or contain itself. To return to Scharmer's idea, perhaps it is an example of art being a way of helping the system "sense and see [and hear] itself". And perhaps another perspective is to see the track representing a parallel process of the wider societal context and *Zeitgeist* out of which it was born. Like our organizations, works of art are permeable and connected to the wider systems within which they sit, not bounded and separate, as we are often tempted to think. They will inevitably play back and echo certain aspects of what is going on around them; the light, and the darkness.

Our organizations are constantly flowing through patterns of escalation and de-escalation. Assuming that an organization is inert, and that stability is inevitable, can be risky. Understanding the dynamics of power can help us choose change or keep things as they are.

No. 5 "Flamenco Sketches" – the sensibility of the bricoleur

The final track on *Kind of Blue* was an exception in the sense that it was recorded in two takes not one. The frame set by Davis was also a little more involved, consisting of a progression through 5 different modal scales at points to be determined by the group in the moment. In particular the Phrygian mode lends this work a southern Spanish sound reflected in the title. And for us this speaks to a quality we have been calling the sensibility of the bricoleur. Davis and his close coterie were influenced widely by jazz, classical and world music genres alike. Davis started classical music training at the establishment Juilliard School of Music before quitting to dedicate himself to New York's jazz clubs. Yet he and his friend and long-time collaborator Gil Evans shared a love of Bartók, Schoenberg, Stravinsky and Debussy which they'd discuss late into the night at Evans' apartment after gigs. At the time in the US there had also been an upsurge in public interest in flamenco culture from Spain. All of this seems to be in the melting pot on this final track of the album; the Spanish nuance of the Phrygian (perhaps heralding the album *Sketches of Spain* that Davis would record later that year), the fleeting nebulous sprays of chords reminiscent of Debussy. There is an openness and curiosity to what there is to experience in the world, which sees them reach beyond their "category"; beyond their professional specialism.

We see this as a characteristic of Bateson's work too in the sense that he moves freely across disciplinary divides. He is open to following the energy of his curiosity. He is attuned to patterns and processes and to the possibility of new thinking if these patterns are taken from their accepted sphere of application and "tried on" elsewhere. Having sometimes struggled to find an academic "home" as a result of this openness, Bateson became an active participant in the series of Macy Conferences that ran from the early 40's through to the 60's. Founded to tackle the problem of "disciplinary isolation" as an impediment to successful medical research, they evolved into a forum for interdisciplinary and transdisciplinary thinking. Intuitively, the bricoleur in both Davis and Bateson was constantly on the look-out for new perspectives that could be combined to make something new and valuable. And if we think about our experiences in organizations too, the threat of disciplinary isolation can loom large. And the good intentions of process optimization and best practice can lead to entrained thinking and *stuckness* over time. Who do we have around us that has that sensibility of the bricoleur, searching magpie-like for the difference that may just make the difference when we most need it?

Staying curious and open to new ideas and half-ideas from other fields can help us avoid getting stuck in old patterns and siloed thinking.

The world in a grain of sand...

We consider the above to be "thought experiments", discursive in nature, perhaps difficult to follow at times. They are of a different nature to the ordered sequential logic of what Heron and Reason (2008, p. 367) might call propositional knowing. They are born of a metaphorical process. Not all of the associations may be useful, but all of them were unexpected and new to us. And it is this instinct that we wanted to claim as part of our practice, and encourage others to have faith in. As a child, Gregory Bateson grew up in a family home which had a number of William Blake's engravings on the walls. We see a commonality between the idea of seeing "the world in a grain of sand", (the quote from his *Auguries of Innocence* which opened the book (Blake, 1994, p.127)), and the Batesonian notion of looking for the "pattern which connects" (Bateson, 2002, p. 7). There is a belief here in a patterned and connected universe, where everything has something to tell us about everything else; and that learning is as much about curiosity as it is about deductive (or reductive) logic. In this spirit, let us go forward.

4

Explorations in sound

We have been trained to think of patterns, with the exception of those of music, as fixed affairs. It is easier and lazier that way but, of course, all nonsense.

Gregory Bateson

You might like to read this while listening to:

Stolen Moments, Oliver Nelson

So, we've traced the work of others (social construction-ists, Gestaltists, complexity thinkers, and the like) to arrive at the idea of organizations as "complex ensemble improvi-sations" (Shaw, 2002, p. 96) where the concept of organi-zational sound becomes an interesting route into exploring options for organizational change. And we've claimed music as "patterned sound in time", a heightened form of sound.

And Bateson and Blake are at our backs assuring us that in curiosity is learning.

Encouraged by this, we have been working for a number of years now on organizational challenges using sound and music as ***an interpretive and exploratory frame***.

Why might sound be interesting?

We have already noted the apparent dominance of visual metaphors over metaphors involving the other senses (and particularly sound). However, if we look further back we find people working actively with other sensory perspectives. The ancient Greek philosopher Pythagoras (570 – 495 BC) discovered that there was an inversely proportional relationship between the lengths of vibrating strings and the pitch of the musical notes that they produced. From this he extrapolated an ordering theory of relationships between celestial bodies that he referred to as the music of the spheres. In these melodic and harmonic relationships, he began to hear the underpinning pattern of the universe. 6th century (AD) Roman philosopher Boethius extended these ideas with his concepts of *musica mundana* (the equivalent of the music of the spheres), *musica humana* (the resonance of these harmonies within the human system), and *musica instrumentalis* (the practice of intervening in harmonies with instruments). And in 1619 German philosopher Johannes Kepler is still working with these ideas and publishes his *Harmonices Mundi* (*The Harmony of the World*, Kepler, 1619). Kepler also explores the idea of relationships between harmonic frequencies being a key organizing principle, though by now his use of the term harmony has broadened beyond tonal frequency, to include pattern, order, relationship and congruence in nature.

More recently, both Kepler and Pythagoras's work is picked up in Bernt Capra's 1990 film, *Mindwalk* (Capra, 1990). The movie centres around three key characters, a physicist, a politician and a poet. Even the set-up is a cast of characters ("poets and birdwatchers") that Bateson would have been pleased to join! In their conversations they range widely across and in between topics known to them, and not known to them, making connections that couldn't have been made, were the conversation partners not from diverse fields. Building on ideas from Pythagoras and Kepler, and using the example of a chord played on a church organ, they arrive at the idea that "the essential nature of matter lies not in objects but in interconnections". The chord as a sum of its notes, has a quality which the individual notes do not have. For example an e ♭ in combination with a c and a g evokes a minor key, something which an e ♭ on its own does not. It is the relationship which makes the harmony. And in a similar way, it is the relationship between time and pitch which makes melody. "Relationships make music" the characters conclude. Reversing this "equation" as it were, if we pay real attention to the music and sounds around us, perhaps this is a portal into understanding the relationships that produce them.

In the beginning was the... sound?
In the Buddhist, Hindu and Jain traditions the sound

Om (or sometimes broken into its constituent vowel sounds A-U-M) is a sacred sound which is in and of the beginnings and fundaments of the universe itself. It is used practically as an incantatory device in various meditation traditions. And also operates at a very deep symbolic level to stand for and generate these deeply patterned frequencies. Western science speaks of the universe beginning with a "big BANG". In Vedic traditions this big bang was a "big OM". First written down and referred to in the Upanishads (800 – 200 BC) this primordial sound is the unleashing of a frequency which allowed the universe to emerge from pure silence; the ultimate "pattern that connects" (Bateson, 2002, p. 7).

If we think of other beginnings too, such as the beginning of human life in the womb, a baby's ears develop far earlier than its eyes. At around nine weeks indentations appear where the baby's ears will be, and they hear their first sounds at around 18 weeks. Their hearing is fully developed before they are even born, whilst their vision is still developing significantly after they are born.

So, the first sensory world they inhabit (and we inhabited) is fundamentally patterned by sound. Pitched sound from outside the womb. And rhythms from within the mother's body; her heartbeat; her breathing. The pattern of relative sound and silence of day and night, sleep and wakefulness. We develop this sense significantly before sight and vision. And this head-start seems to persist. Even for adults with 20/20 vision, our average field of vision is 120 degrees; whilst we can hear in 360 degrees.

On eyes and ears...

Johann Wolfgang von Goethe is probably best known today as a poet and playwright, the writer of the *Faust* tragedies, and of countless lyric poems which are at the heart of European Romantic literature. He is less well known for his scientific work. His tradition of science was very much rooted in experiencing phenomena in the world and nature, and working intuitively to develop insight from these experiences. The scientific tradition that we are more familiar with these days is the theoretical model, whereby a hypothesis is developed and then taken to the outside world to be proven or disproven. In his 1810 work *Sketch of a Theory of Colours* Goethe works *from* his experience of light and colour towards a theory. Picking up on a subject that Sir Isaac Newton had already looked into close to a century before, he seems to reverse the direction of the inquiry; and in these reversals makes some interesting assertions:

"The eye may be said to owe its existence to light, which calls forth, as it were, a sense that is akin to itself; the eye, in short, is formed with reference to light, to be fit for the action of light; the light it contains corresponding with the light without."

(Goethe, [1810] (1840) p. xxxix)

Because the phenomenon of light exists, the eye develops;

rather than light being perceptible to us because the eye exists. It seems like a surprising reversal. However, if we follow the whim and pursue a parallel example, then because the phenomenon of sound exists, the ear develops. And if the first event in the universe was sonic in nature, be it the "big BANG" or the "big OM", then the sense of hearing and the auditory, would seem to have a fundamental significance which is not proportionate with the attention we give to it in our organizational lives.

From hearing to listening

It's not a perfect definition but often hearing is characterized as a more passive perception of sound, whereas listening is active (perhaps paralleled by seeing and looking); a deliberate, focused act, that may be the precursor to proportionate (patterned?) response in any given context. This too is an old idea, and for us always brings to mind the Senecan story, *The Listener* (Shaw, 2018). Here, an unruly boy is sent by the village to a wild uncle who lives on the edge of the forest. The boy is too much for the village to handle, and it is said that the uncle is the only one who will know what to do. The boy arrives at his uncle's hut with notions of the glory of hunting day in and day out. Instead the uncle sends him into the forest to find a great tree to sit under, and listen to the sounds and rhythms of what goes on. He does this every day for four years, in the tutelage of the patterns of the lands beyond the village. In the story that follows he goes on to face considerable hardship and duress; but it is the resources and relationships he has built up during his years of listening that see him through. Ultimately, he leads a group of men who become the founding fathers of a tribal network of their people.

Listening as a pre-requisite for responding appropriately comes to the fore in Western European myth tradition in stories of Parzival (Shaw, 2018) and the grail legend. The first time Parzival finds his way to the Grail Castle he is told about and shown many things by the Grail King and his entourage. He hears and sees but is stricken with anxiety about what is expected of him. Voices from the past echo around his head and counsel silence. And the land falls to grief again. Many years of suffering and reflection later see Parzival once more confronted with the Grail King. With the experience of the years, he is able to listen to what he is being told and respond from his own wisdom, to ask the Grail King the question that allows recovery to begin in the land and the culture.

Listening as the ideal state for responding

In a more contemporary context, listening is at the heart of a number of improvisational practices, in theatre and in music. In improvisational theatre, players are striving to stay in the state of the second Parzival, where they are attentive to what is going on in the moment, and responding from their own truths. Experience on the stage teaches that there is enough novel and disruptive information in any live interaction to let you make the next move in the scene. When anxiety kicks in though, improv teams talk about having to guard against "pre-thought". This is the moment when they notice they are not listening to what is happening on stage, and are responding to voices in their heads telling them to think of something clever, something funny, or introduce "disruption". If this takes hold, then the scene can quickly end somewhere called "crazytown", where the situation is built from disconnected ideas thrown out by players no longer listening to each other and responding in the moment (or worse, gags or lines that have been "pre-thought"). These scenes lack the emergent patterning that is the result of true listening. They are less satisfying to play, and to watch. And even an "unschooled" improv audience will pick up on the lack of life. "Comedy" in this context (and elsewhere) often comes from fulfilling or interrupting patterns. And when the interactions are random not patterned, at some deep level, we know.

And we see this in organizational life too. How often have we been part of meetings where much of what has been said has been "pre-thought"? Colleagues arrive at the Monday morning conference call at the allotted time to deliver information when their turn comes, before retreating back onto mute and into a passive state. Information is exchanged but no one is truly listening or changed by what they hear.

And the inner voices that Parzival and our players hear, are also alive and well in organization. In psychological terms you could equate these to introjects from our upbringing and socialization. These are the voices from our past that can make themselves heard at times of pressure. The softly whispered "you're going to mess this up" before the big presentation; the stern "you need to hurry up and get this sorted" as the deadline approaches. Reviewed in a positive light they could be seen as voices looking to protect us. However, what is clear is that they are based on information from past situations, not information in the here and now. Our organizational lives are increasingly complex. In a complex system, interactions are dynamic, and cause and effect not plannable (much like an improv scene). In this context, only information from the present can give us a sense of what the appropriate response might be. Learning to listen, much like in the Senecan tale, would seem to be a fundamental leadership skill.

And it is hard. Moving to the world of musical improvisation now, jazz bassist and composer Charles Mingus visualizes this struggle in his autobiographical work *Beneath the Underdog* (Mingus, 1998). He sees his personality as three characters, almost viewed at a reflective distance as if on a stage. There is the one who is anxious and whose instinct is to hide. There is the one who is easily angered and whose instinct is to destroy. And there is the third who wants to listen. This is the musician Mingus, trying to find his way in to the state where he can listen and create in the moment, not be snarled up by the fight and flight triggers from a difficult past. This striking image from the very first pages of the book really frame his career and experiences as a struggle to get out of his own way. This is probably true in some respects for all of us, but Mingus displays a level of raw honesty that doesn't often make it across the corporate threshold. In the story of Parzival, his failure to ask the question the first time around is due to "the instinct being bred out of him". Somewhere along the way the chivalric codes and culture of the Arthurian court have gotten in the way of a true response to the situation he faces. And we see this in a number of forms in organization too, for example, the search for creativity and innovation. Organizations often seek to learn creativity from external sources, courses, workshops, innovation processes etc; when really you could view it as an instinct which has been bred out of our organizational patterns. The source of the disruptive information we need to make the next creative response is there in the moment, if we can listen in order to hear. Acknowledging that we are allowing our metaphors to slip, we are back with Blake, learning to "see a world in a grain of sand / and a heaven in a wild flower", skills we would do well to cultivate.

On the listening state

At the risk of contradicting ourselves, the listening state can also be seen as having more to it than just learning to respond to what is going on in the moment. Organizational theorist Claudio Ciborra talks about the improvisational (or listening and responding) mode as being one where our past experiences and skills are brought to bear on the current situation in a helpful way (Ciborra, 1999). In his thinking, the phenomenology of the improvisational moment is not *just* what is going on the moment. There are echoes into the moment from the past, and the first sensings into what might be in the future too. There is a slender metaphorical "bubble" which also holds some of what was, and what is yet to be. He talks about harnessing these skilfully as being part of the "wisdom of systems", which we are connecting as we write with the wisdom that Parzival attains in the lost years before he finds his way back to the Grail Castle. The trick is finding a way to bring our experience into the present moment in a way that supports how we choose to respond to what we are hearing, rather than trips us up.

This is a "tight-rope walk" at the heart of the practice of jazz musicians. Organizational consultant and jazz musician Frank Barrett writes extensively on this in his *Yes to the Mess: Surprising Leadership Lessons from Jazz* (Barrett, 2012, pp. 121-123). For Barrett, key skills include "comping" and "generous listening". Comping is acting to support the lines "spoken" by fellow musicians, with a view to making one another look good. And the prerequisite for this is attentive listening with positive regard. But this is all for nothing if the technical experience on the instrument is not there too in the moment, or the agreement about what tune is being played. However, whilst bringing their experience into each improvisational moment, jazz musicians are on their guard for *too much*prior experience. If standard licks, riffs or phrases occur too often, the improvisational quality of listening and responding "live" dissipates, and we notice this in the quality of the music.

Working with the sound metaphor in organization
So, having immersed ourselves in these associations and connections, a number of sources and traditions seem to be encouraging us to take sound and listening seriously. In an organizational context, if we accept that each organization has

its own "sound" made up of the unique voices that are part of it and the unique conversations they are having, then the idea of "re-sounding organizations" becomes a frame for working to hear what is going on, and finding ways to experiment with different choices.

In our work we found "sound" a little too high-level a term to use practically. It was too easy to slip into abstract discussions about organization, rather than connect it to specific actions and interactions in the here and now. So knowing that (as a colleague of ours is fond of saying) all models are wrong and some are helpful, we broke the idea of "musical sound" down into 4 key parts to make it easier to pay attention to what is going on:

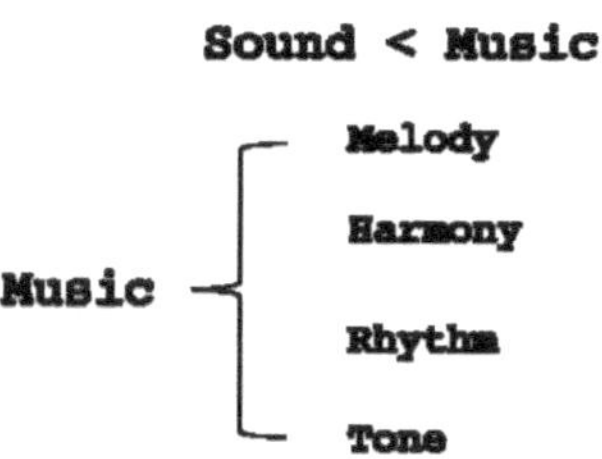

Rather than being categories or buckets into which organizational life should be parsed and analysed, we'd encourage you to hold them lightly as metaphors for making sense of what is going on. To give you an idea, what follows are some of the connections we make with these terms.

Melody

We connect melody most closely with the idea of individual voices speaking into organizations. Our individual melody lines might be the ideas we articulate, the thinking and narratives we present, our suggestions for organizational ways forward. There are rare moments when we get an opportunity for a solo melodic line, perhaps a formal key-note speech, or exploring a new idea with a coach deeply attuned to listening. However, in most instances our individual melodies will sooner or later be met with responses from the rest of the "band". If this is not to end in organizational cacophony, we must become skilled at hearing and responding to other people's melody lines. In musical terms organizational life is contrapuntal, a weaving in and out of different melodic units. And innovative, agile organizations find ways of allowing this polyvocality, this mix of different voices, to thrive; for each voice to be heard and have influence on the melodic whole. Paying attention to the idea of melodic lines in our meetings and other organizational interactions can help us see where melodies are clashing, and notice where musical themes (melodies) are being lost and not developed.

Harmony

It is possible for individual voices to outline a dominant harmony, however, we hear harmonies in organizations most clearly when there are multiple voices involved, and the chords are fully populated. One way of thinking of harmony is as the tonal context that helps us make sense of individual notes. The note e ♭ played in the tonal context of a

C minor chord will have a particular effect. The same note played in the tonal context of an E ♭ major chord will have a different effect. Much as identical individual suggestions and leadership acts can have a different impact depending on the "harmonic context". We've all had the experience of the same idea or suggestion being rejected as a wrong note at a certain point in a meeting, whilst being received with great recognition at a later point.

Another way of thinking about harmony is as the dominant mood or "weather", the organizational climate which can shift and change. At a very basic level is the organization / team playing in a major or minor key? Where multiple moods and weathers are at play, there can be conflict or discord where fronts meet. Either way, it is helpful to develop the skill to hear the underlying harmonies in an organizational context or indeed conversation, rather than just focusing on the individual notes.

Rhythm

We think of rhythm most often as the usual pace of organizational life. It's often made up of ordered patterns, regular routines, standard processes, things that happen at certain times of the day or week. There is something about the rhythm which underpins and steadies organizational life. And at times a rhythm can be so driving and relentless that it is difficult to change direction; or it becomes so loud that it drowns out ideas or possibilities of new directions of exploration. In a changing organizational context, the driving rhythm could be the view that says "we've always done it this way", or "keep your head down and carry on".

Over time, rhythms are more interesting if they draw attention to themselves through variations. Changes in rhythm keep the musicians on their toes, making sure they are attending to each other in the moment rather than sleepwalking through the steady 4/4 of the last five years of organizational life. In the same way, practising shifts in the rhythm of our regular meetings, or daily routines can really help us stay alive to what we are doing, and check that we are playing to the right rhythm. And even if we do choose to return to the steady 4/4 after a time, then it is at least enlivened by the departure.

Tone

The tone of a singer or instrumentalist is often the quality that makes them uniquely identifiable. Something of their character, their experiences, their life choices, what they stand for is revealed in the timbre of their singing or playing. It can be the grit that comes out in that inflected blue note every now and again; or that soft vibrato that somehow supports and understands. It seems to tap into all the singer or player's broad experiences, and bring them to bear in *this* specific performance now.

And it is tone that we can also bring to our leading and acting into organizations. It takes time to develop. And it has to do with connecting in a broader way to what we are doing in organizations, from a societal or ethical perspective, not just the narrow perspective of an individual organization's success (in whatever terms these are framed). When we are caught up in the pace of the organizational rhythm, or preoccupied with weaving our melodies, it is a leader leading with their own distinct "tone" that can help us step back and ask those important questions about purpose, and what our actions are in service of. Tone is something role-modelled through the way we act and lead in organization, and has something of wisdom; elderhood even. And these wider perspectives are not only a check and balance, they can also provide the angle to see, hear and respond appropriately to the disruptive and unexpected.

Working in practice

In the next section of this book we dive deeper into the concepts of melody, harmony, rhythm and tone; and look at examples of working with this metaphorical framework in practice. Each chapter begins with a definition of the term in question. This is our opening musical theme, if you like. We then riff on and explore connections and variations within this text / theme, before moving into a number of practical organizational examples to give these connections an applied context. These sections are marked with the following icon for ease of reference:

The flow of ideas is deliberately associative rather than following a specifically linear logic, so feel free to dip in and out of the "working in practice" sections in a different order if you prefer (there is an overview of the topics in the Appendix). Rather than being a restrictive blueprint, our hope is that these examples help you generate other ideas about how you might explore the sound metaphor in practice in your own organizational contexts.

A note on diagnostic and dialogic perspectives
We are conscious of the trap of frameworks that oversimplify, seem to offer an easy way of diagnosing situations, and miss the life of interactions in the process. We know that in many ways assembling the ingredients of melody, harmony, rhythm and tone does not result in music; there is more going on.

We offer these metaphors as a frame for exploring the richness of organizational life. As we experienced in holding Miles Davis's *Kind of Blue* alongside Bateson's *Steps to an Ecology of Mind*, there is something about working with metaphoric processes that can get at things we might not otherwise reach. We hope this is a route into dialogue rather than an end in itself.

In his third novel, *Still Life with Woodpecker*, Tom Robbins explores society from an outlaw's perspective, and lights on a similar subject. We share this with a wry smile as an over-blown version of a truth:

"The problem starts at the secondary level, not with the originator or developer of the idea but with the people who are attracted by it, who adopt it, who cling to it until their last nail breaks, and who invariably lack the overview, flexibility, imagination, and most importantly, sense of humor, to maintain it in the spirit in which it was hatched. Ideas are made by masters, dogma by disciples. There is a particularly unattractive and discouragingly common affliction called tunnel vision, which, for all the misery it causes, ought to top the job list at the World Health Organization…when a good idea is run through the filters and compressors of ordinary tunnel vision, it not only comes out reduced in scale and value but in its new dogmatic configuration produces effects the opposite of those for which it was originally intended"

(Robbins, 1980, pp. 85-86)

We don't necessarily subscribe to the stridency of the tone, but there is also truth in the point. And our invitation here is to play with the music and sound metaphor as a possible route to finding out interesting things, and not as a truth in its own right.

A note on slippery metaphors

And whilst you are playing, we feel duty bound to alert you again to a professional hazard. We've already noted that the lure of the visual metaphor is everywhere. And we have found that when we are working with the sound metaphor, other metaphors (particularly but not only visual) constantly creep in. We've noticed a purist urge in ourselves to purge our language of "erroneous" metaphor and stick to the language of sound. And then smiled at our own incongruence as we see ourselves shoring up one perspective in a book that at its heart is pleading for the power of holding multiple perspectives. So a word of warning: your metaphors will slip. That's OK, go with it and be interested in the mix!

Melody

You might like to read this while listening to:

Autumn Leaves, Cannonball Adderley

Theme

One of the things that connects us is that, from our days as school boy musicologists, dog-eared copies of *The Grove Dictionary of Music* still grace both our bookshelves. Consulting this oracle from the past we read that:

Melody, defined as pitched sounds arranged in musical time in accordance with given cultural conventions and constraints, represents a universal human phenomenon traceable to prehistoric times...

(Melody, *The Grove Dictionary of Music*, 2020)

Hearing this we are thinking back to Patricia Shaw's idea of organization as "ensemble improvisation" (Shaw, 2002, p. 96), and the fact that there may be multiple people contributing "pitched sounds" to the melody, multiple melody lines, or indeed "theme and variation" where the initial melody line is modified over time by alternative voices and instruments. The definition speaks to the universality of music as a human experience, which we have already touched on, supporting the idea of it as a fundamental patterning that we may discern if we develop (or rediscover) the ears to hear. And the idea of convention and constraint also seems deeply relevant to our organizational experience. In Stacey's exploration of the idea of organizations as "complex responsive processes" much significance is given to the effect of power and constraint. In theory we are free to respond to the gestures others make in organizational life in any way we see fit. In practice, how we respond in the moment is shaped by things like our perceptions of relative power. This influences which gestures and responses get amplified in our organizational patterning, and which get dampened. So, a melodic gesture in an organizational context could be a recommendation or suggestion from a hierarchical leader in a team. The influence of power possibly increases the likelihood of it being heard as a melody by other players, and repeated. If the hierarchical influence is very strong, and there is fear in the system, then the melodic line may be repeated over and over, with the risk of monotony or entrenchment in the team's melody (or thinking). In a team environment with more of a balance of power, the melody line might be picked up, altered, and developed (innovated).

And thinking of this from the other end of the power spectrum, what melodic contributions might be ventured pianissimo, and overheard in the near unison repetitions of the dominant themes in any organization? There is often valuable difference and variety that we are missing if we are not attuned to picking up these melodic fragments. And the challenge is that they won't always be there to be heard; people will simply stop playing them. Over time, these patterns of amplification and dampening settle into what we might call the (conversational) culture of a team. We learn what notes can be played, and what can't. We constrain ourselves and each other to the melodic context that we have learned is safe. It might be harmonious for a time, but the risk of monotony and stagnation is never far.

Variation: Finding your tune…

We vividly remember our early experiences of singing in choirs. The first songs are usually in unison, and you can follow others with confidence and safety in numbers. Gradually pieces with multiple lines are introduced. And that's when we started to feel really exposed. We remember trying to hold our own melodic lines and frequently being lured onto the rocks of other people's melody lines. It felt like we had to develop an aural musculature and hold it in place in order to keep to our own line; learn to ride the tensions of the counterpoint. It required encouragement and experience to trust that holding our own line would not lead to harmonic disaster; that we could sing with our own voices and still produce something coherent together.

And this experience speaks to us quite strongly of the process of finding and developing our voices in organizations as leaders, followers, participants. Later in his career, trumpeter and flugelhornist Clark Terry became heavily involved in jazz education as part of the US school system. On the one hand, he was keen to make a contribution to the furthering of the art form. On the other hand, he could see the benefits of his experience of learning and growing through collective music-making stretching beyond the purely musical context. There was something about community and collaboration that students could learn from the jazz experience which could help them in other collective contexts. And he did much to support the idea of music as something that is deliberately learnt, a craft more than a heaven-sent gift of the muses. He framed musical development as three phases: "imitate, assimilate, innovate" (Terry, 2007, p. 258). In the early stages, find your role models and teachers and try out what they do. Don't worry about being "original" to begin with. Over time, with deliberate practice, you'll integrate what they have to teach you, assimilate it into something that is more and more your own melodic voice. Over time, from this assimilated platform, with the technique and craft you have built up along the way, you are in a position to develop something new. Melodic innovation here is not random creation, it draws on what went before, on listening and learning from others. In an organizational context, the equivalent is perhaps framing leadership as a deliberate, reflective practice; a coming into our own voices, with work, over time.

Variation: What can get in the way of this?

Other people's voices

Whilst the process Clark Terry describes is very deliberate, for most of us, finding our own melodic lines can be a more haphazard affair, with plenty of advances as well as backslides on the way. Gestalt writers Herman and Korenich talk about the concept of "oughts and shoulds". These are voices from the past that we hear at times, and that try and influence how we act in the present (Herman & Korenich, 1977, pp. 43-46). They often hold echoes of dominant voices from key phases of our development and socialization as children, frequently parents, guardians, teachers, community leaders. In psychological terms they are introjected ideals, which can hold us up to a standard from the past, which may or may not be the most helpful for us in any given moment. We "shouldn't waste our time with this new project, it'll never work anyway"; or "we ought to work late or the boss will be angry". They are often originally voices that sought to protect us; but in adulthood they can get in the way of us finding our own melodic line in response to what is actually happening. We end up playing bits of other people's melodies rather than our own.

Too many voices

This is a phenomenon that can occur with many instruments, but in our experience we've seen it most commonly with guitarists. The journey begins with an acoustic guitar. At some point, an electric guitar is added, probably solid-bodied, Fender style. Then comes the first effects pedal. Then the next. Then possibly the semi-acoustic jazz guitar and some more pedals. Lots of effects and voices are tried out, over months, probably years. Yet still the sound is like catching snatches of other people playing. Often a really authentic guitar style starts to come through when some or most of these other voices are dropped in favour of something simpler. And in the career of many famous guitarists the journey goes back to the original acoustic, but arrived at in a different way. We can see parallels to this in organizations too. Leadership development and the MBA programmes at business schools across the world provide leaders with hundreds of models and approaches, toolkits and strategic frameworks to help them with their organizational challenges. The intent may be honourable, but actually much of what we give leaders along the way are the excess effects pedals. Really finding an authentic way of leading and working with others is the journey beyond the effects pedals back to something simpler, more immediate, felt.

Letting go enough

In the prologue to his book on improvisation in life and art, *Free Play*, Stephen Nachmanovitch quotes a folk tale about a young flute player who apprentices himself to a master (Nachmanovitch, 1990, pp. 1-3). He applies himself and studies hard for a number of years, yet the master always finds something lacking in his playing. Eventually, in frustration, he leaves his home village for the anonymity of the capital city, runs out of money, starts drinking and for a long time ekes out an existence of real hardship. Many, many years later, he chances back to the village where the master flautist is giving a concert with his apprentices. Our man, in a mix of trance and shame, goes along to the gathering, and has the opportunity to play. He has let go of any expectations of pleasing others, and, for the first time plays, in the words of the master, "like a god". There seems to be something important about letting all of our experiences count in finding our own melody lines; and letting go of ideals of what we want to or "ought" to be. If we can get out of our own way, we might stand a chance of playing our own tunes with others, in the here and now, which is to be as effective as we can be.

Working in practice: Melody in teams

Some years ago we worked with a senior leadership team in an industrial manufactur-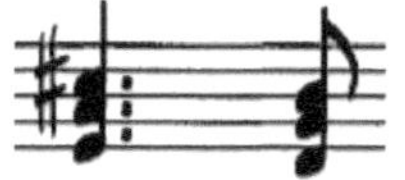ing organization. Competition in its market places meant that pressure had been building to find ways of innovating (from industrial processes to marketing practices, to commercial pricing). The leader of the team had expressed frustration that, as a group, they were not coming up with new ideas fast enough, and that he felt more and more pressure to come up with ideas on behalf of the group. Having spoken to all members of the team individually, it became clear that conversely, some team members were finding it difficult to contribute ideas in team conversations as they felt the leader dominated the conversations. We observed a number of their meetings and indeed noticed how this pattern played out. The senior leader had a style of exploring his thinking out loud. At times we would hear others starting to speak, or notice an intake of breath or a cough as people prepared to say something; and yet despite this the senior leader would take off on a train of thought again. We explored this with the group afterwards. A number of team members expressed that they had tried to add to the conversation, but had not been "let in", or had been "talked over". They felt stifled, and unable to bring or develop their ideas. The senior leader, however, explained that he hadn't noticed others trying to speak. He felt he was leaving gaps between his thoughts for others to get in. Then, when there was, what he experienced as, yawning silence, he felt the burden of having to continue on his own, as he thought no one else was there to support.

This put us in mind of John Coltrane playing with a group Miles Davis had put together. It's common practice for jazz musicians to take turns playing solos, improvising on the melody and developing it before handing over to the next soloist. However, somehow Coltrane had gotten into the habit of taking chorus after chorus and soloing for long periods of time. Each time he got to the end of a 32 bar section and others were ready to come in he would just keep playing and go round again. When confronted about this Coltrane said that each time he came to the end of a chorus he didn't know how to stop, he didn't know how to get his musical thinking to a place where he felt ok to let a pause in. Miles's droll advice was "just take the horn out of your mouth".

Now this anecdote is not an exact parallel for what was going on in the team we were working with. However, the senior leader's style of thinking out loud, and anxiety about carrying the whole burden for generating new ideas, had led to a pattern of him "overplaying". Like Coltrane, he was struggling with letting in the pauses, anxious that the responsibility for the continuing development of the music fell solely to him, and that if he stopped playing, the inevitable disaster would be his fault.

Having spotted this pattern, and become curious about it as a group, we were able to frame some small conversational experiments. The senior leader experimented with pausing more deliberately after sharing his thoughts and ideas – holding in mind a sense of the small silences at the end of musical phrases or choruses. At first, he found the silences uncomfortable and reverted to old habits, but we were able to notice this as a group and recalibrate the experiment. Others in the group conversely experimented with being more definitive in giving audible cues that they were keen to speak. Because of the positional power of the senior leader, some members of the team had noticed feeling that it was not OK to "interrupt" so the deliberate form of this as a conversational experiment helped them have the permission to speak their thoughts more forcefully into the group. The change was by no means immediate. The "sound" of their conversations as they practiced new ways of speaking together was jolty at first. However, with practice, the balance shifted. The share of voice was distributed more evenly. More and different melodic lines and ideas began to come to the fore. The musical lines became more subtle and generative as they built on each others' ideas and felt less individual responsibility for coming up with the whole melody on their own. And, when old habits died hard, we have heard that a good natured "take the horn out of your mouth" was all the corrective that was needed.

Working in practice: Hearing the counter-tune

A corporate counselling business had been overhauling its systems and procedures with a view to increasing governance, over-sight, and efficiency, as its operations grew. 
Amongst other initiatives, a board review had identified a need to reduce the average counselling time for clients from 28 to 26 minutes to increase the commercial viability of the organization. They were aware that this might not be a uni-versally popular move, so decided that they would hold an open consultation forum, where colleagues were invited to share their views. At this forum, one of the counselling staff shared that they found the suggested time reduction frustrat-ing. They had gone into the profession with a passion for helping clients, and they felt that increasingly the organiza-tion was taking them away from the work which was at the core of their identity and purpose. If time was a constraint, they shared that they and a colleague had just spent two days (or 960 minutes) trying to fix a problem which had arisen through the rushed implementation of a new IT system. In the counsellor's view reducing some of the burden of back of-fice processes on their time would be a route to achieving even more time saving, without the detriment to the client, and the

risk that they perceived this to hold. Whilst the counsellor had been speaking the managing director had become visibly agitated. He gruffly asserted that the decision to implement the system in question had been taken and that was the last he wanted to hear about it. A valid melody line which came from a place of integrity and customer-centricity had just been closed down. What's more, the managing director's actions at an open forum had just sent a strong message that alternative melody lines, or counter-tunes were not welcome. Whilst the forum was an espoused attempt to demonstrate an openness to hearing what others have to say, the agitated reaction and drowning out of the counter-tune was a message that all heard loud and clear.

On the contrary, design thinker Kees Dorst (2015) talks about how organizations who are looking to adapt and develop need to find ways of embracing alternative melodies and counter-tunes if they are not to stagnate. Working from their old melodies, all organizations can do is tinker and embellish around the edges of their existing themes. Rising to adaptive challenges in disruptive markets requires hearing and allowing alternative themes to be stated and developed. One example he gives is of using the metaphor of a music festival to help a local government group understand the complex patterns of late-night crime and overcrowding in a club district. This choice of metaphor focused attention not only on the individual businesses themselves, but also on the richness of the wider system of the night time economy in the city (like the multiple stalls and stages of a music festival), with its multiple harmonious and discordant themes and variations. This led to a fuller understanding of the influences at play, and of the choices the group had for intervening. The approach may seem unusual, but it opened up routes to newness and innovation in the group's thinking. It speaks to an instinct we see in Miles Davis too, who was always on the lookout for individual players with a unique voice who he could bring into his band, knowing that better musical choices would be the result. And this is something that Barrett notices more widely in jazz around innovation as the power of bringing in what we would call the "unusual suspects" to foster variety and progress (Barrett, 2012, pp. 67-92). This is an instinct that was not present (or got closed down) in the corporate counselling example above. The counter-tune had so much to do with professional identity and passion that it did not disappear altogether, rather went underground. Significant bad feeling and resistance were felt as a result of the act of public silencing, and struggles with employee engagement and morale increased.

Working in practice: The human note

We worked alongside a Business to Consumer service business that was in the process of transforming many of its customer interactions into a digital context. Digital trans-formation was the buzz word on everyone's lips, and had somehow become an undeniable truth, a dominant melody; it was the "obvious way to go". However, in private conversations with individuals we'd heard a note of loss creep in at times. As a customer service business, many employees had joined as they enjoyed the human contact with customers, and "giving the personal touch" was, for many, a source of pride. What we noticed was that the dominance of the metaphor of "going digital" had somehow disappeared some of the warmth of the human touch that was a real differentiator for the business. The challenge was, that it seemed impossible to "keep the human touch" whilst "going digital". These two themes appeared to be mutually exclusive.

What helped here was exploring examples of combining these two ideas. We were put in mind of Jimi Hendrix and his use of the technology of the wah-wah pedal to create wailing guitar sounds, with a deeply human quality to them. And we thought of fellow guitarist Peter Frampton's talk box. This was a device he invented which channelled digital sounds from his guitar's amplifier via a tube into the cavities of his mouth, where he could modify them through shaping his cheeks and lips – literally adding the human touch. Neither of these were exactly "solutions" to the challenge faced in this digital transformation. However, as examples that suggested that "digital" and "human" were not irreconcilable, we were able to use these to start a conversation about what a service model that kept the best of both might look like.

In a different expression of this, we worked in a pharmaceutical research company with groups of back office staff (accounting, purchase ledger, IT support and so on). The view amongst this group was that the real "melody makers" in the organization were the frontline researchers in labs around the world, developing techniques and medicines to help people in need. At times, they struggled to feel that they were contributing to the music. They worked in small back-office locations dotted around, and had little sense of what the overall organization was achieving. The organization decided to bring this group together at an event that would allow them to hear what was going on more widely in other areas of the business. Through this they were able to reconnect with their part in the whole. They were able to realize afresh, that whilst their roles were about good process and procedures, and not literally saving lives in the frontline, that carrying out these back-office functions was vital in allowing the organization to operate. The emphasis on process and procedure in their roles had left them feeling detached from the very human melody of the organization as a whole, and reconnecting with this was deeply motivating.

Working in practice: Training the listening muscle

We noted above the difficulties we can face in arriving at our own melody lines; our own views, standpoints, truths. The challenge in organizational life is that our melody lines necessarily interact with those of other people. If the result is not to be organizational cacophony, then it's important that we learn how to hear other people's melodies, and adapt to and be changed by them. This is not about allowing ourselves to be dominated; it is not literally about "changing our tune" when we hear something else; it is more about allowing our melodic truths to be altered by others and giving ourselves the space to respond differently. This patterning is very much what Stacey is talking about in his concept of organizations as "complex responsive processes" (Stacey, 2003). The gestures people make are their intentions and actions; and the complexity comes as no one can control how others will respond, or how their intentions and actions might intersect.

Deep listening can help this patterning become generative. And in our work with teams in particular, learning to develop the listening muscle can make a real difference. To help teams get curious about their patterns of interacting with melodies, we often set individual members small tasks. For example, we might ask them, in a specific meeting, or across a window of a few hours in a day, to focus on really hearing the ideas / melodies that are being played by others, before stating their own melodic line. For each idea or suggestion someone makes, we ask them to summarize it (replay it) and check back what they have heard with the individual. We then ask them to find a way of building on that idea with a variation of their own. Following the meeting or the allotted time frame, we invite them to make a few notes on what they have noticed in the conversations. How did the conversational dynamic shift? What variations did they play on others' ideas? How might their melodic line have been altered by this? We then ask them to make an appointment to explore anything that has interested them with the other team members involved. The process sounds quite stop / start when you read it like this, and it can take a little while to get used to; however, what it does is take people out of their instinctive (stuck?) patterns of conversation, and builds in space for curiosity and reflection, both in the moment, and in retrospect. Without being too heavy on the theory, these can be seen as mini cycles of action research inquiry and experimentation (McNiff, 2002). Even if one or two members of a team make small shifts in their modes of interacting in conversations, it can make a big difference to how they interact as a group. With more "listening participants" teams typically report that their conversations are lighter, flow better, and get stuck less often in patterns of opposition. And meetings that people used to dread in the past become more engaging and fruitful.

Working in practice: Melodic metaphor

Sometimes when working with groups it can be helpful to take them away from their own contexts in order to be able to notice their own organizational patterns or team dynamics more clearly. For example, sometimes we introduce them to a short clip of a Michael Jackson stadium concert, where Jackson is playing with Guns N' Roses guitarist Slash. The clip is currently on YouTube here (links may change of course but we imagine this moment will remain searchable):

https://www.youtube.com/watch?v=9lxN7x8JVKM

Jackson and Slash are coming to the coda or finale of a performance of "Black or White". As Jackson and the rest of the band try and draw things to a close, Slash continues to solo on the guitar. Jackson is seen stage left, seemingly becoming more and more irate as Slash holds onto his solo line (and to centre stage), even as roadies try and make him stop.

The clip is just over 2 minutes long. We'll then often simply ask groups what they recognize from what they've just heard in their own organizations. Responses are always rich, varied and insightful; and sometimes name some difficult truths. Things we have heard back from groups include:

- Competitive leadership dynamics – leaders vying for the stage
- Dominant leaders hogging the limelight
- The band as the rest of the team not knowing which leader to follow – whether to stop with Jackson or continue supporting Slash
- A leader who has been replaced in an organization refusing to make way for their successor and disrupting and sabotaging their performance
- The "roadies" representing the supporters of one particular leader in an organization who would be called in to round on anyone stating an opposing view
- Slash's solo as the equivalent of a habit of over-explaining by one Chief Technical Officer which meant meetings dragged on and never came to a satisfactory conclusion
- Slash's solo as the equivalent of someone holding forth in a meeting and when challenged saying "I'm just stat-

ing my perspective" when actually it's an attempt to attack or undermine

- Real fight or staged theatrics? Connections with perceived leadership game-playing at town hall meetings and public events. General sense of mistrust about what happens onstage and offstage in the organization.

We're always surprised and fascinated by the connections people make. We shouldn't be. If Bateson's taught us anything, it's the power of making connections between contexts that the dominant perspective says don't belong together. We feel encouraged to raid the "profane" world of popular music, to learn for the good of the "sacred" world of organization. We'd like to encourage you too.

Concluding thoughts: Towards polyvocality

There are many aspects of melody to consider. And it strikes us that in an organizational context one of the key tensions to manage is that between one's own melody line, and that of the group. Where individuals are only singing for themselves, the risk of organizational cacophony is always near. On the other hand, a group-think unison chorus is not going to make for an adaptable or viable organizational system, particularly in disrupted or complex contexts. The ideal is something we might call polyvocality; a state where all of the voices and voicings in the organizational sound can be heard distinctly, and where the overall melodies adapt and change in response to one another. The pauses and listening in the music-making are as important as contributing notes. They are spaces that allow us to hear the resonance of the unfolding melodies and choose how to respond.

We are making connections to the idea of metacognition from mindfulness and meditative practice; the ability to notice one's thoughts as they are occurring, and be more deliberate in how we respond.

In turn, this makes us think of management researcher David Snowden's work on complexity leadership; and how in a complex context what is required of the leader is exquisite attention to what is going on in the moment, and an almost intuitive sensing into what might be the right next move (Snowden, 2007).

And then we are at the North Sea Jazz Festival in the late 80's with Brazilian percussion player, Naná Vasconcelos. The Henry Threadgill Sextet are in full free jazz flow and Naná is on stage with them. The context is unfamiliar, and he is wondering how to join in. He sways between bouts of anxiety, and moments where he is in tune and sensing what to do. In the 7th minute, he reaches for and plays the bells. It is the only moment he plays, but the timing is perfect.

When we are dealing with complex situations and there are many voices, many melody lines, perhaps our work is to try to be the still centre that hears what is going on, and makes the minimum most effective intervention, rather than thrashing around on the drum kit driven by anxiety or ego.

6

Harmony

You might like to read this while listening to:

Maiden Voyage, Herbie Hancock

Theme

The Grove Dictionary of Music definitions seem to be the creative constraint we've given ourselves, so let's go back to the dog-eared tome for our jumping-off point. Grove describes harmony as:

The combining of notes simultaneously, to produce chords, and successively, to produce chord progressions. The term is used descriptively to denote notes and chords so combined, and also prescriptively to denote a system of structural principles governing their combination.

(Harmony, *The Grove Dictionary of Music*, 2020)

The first aspect of harmony mentioned is that it involves combining notes, or indeed combining sequences of notes (or individual melody lines). What is emphasized here is the importance of the connection or relationship between the notes. Together, these have the potential to create moments with a particular harmonic quality, or indeed moments of disharmony or discordance. Sequences of these moments of relationship can lead to progression, action, movement. And it is these qualities of relationships that we can sometimes miss in organizational life. We've developed a tendency, particularly in Western thought and science, to focus our attention on the separateness of things, and struggle to notice them in their dynamic related contexts. Bateson was fond of using the example of the human hand to highlight the obvious things we miss. When asked to say what they notice when observing the hand most groups responded by identifying the five digits (thumb and four fingers). Bateson would then point out that the essence of the hand from an evolutionary perspective is not five digits, but rather (at least) four sets of relationships (between the thumb and each finger). These opposable pincer relationships were a crucial evolutionary development, giving early humans an advantage in terms of dexterity. The digits in isolation, which seem to be the first thing we notice, would be largely irrelevant without the relationship. Blake also notes the disadvantage of this mode of perception in the epigraph we quoted earlier:

"...he only takes portions of existence and fancies it the whole..."
(William Blake, 1994, p. 185)

Both Blake and Bateson are arguing that relationship is what we should be paying attention to first and foremost, the notes *in combination*, as Grove puts it. And we notice that we struggle with this often in an organizational context. We write job descriptions for individual roles. We label individuals with job titles. We divide our staff into specialist functions. Yet rarely do we spend as much time articulating the existing or desired relationships between individuals, functions, departments as we do in subtly emphasizing their separateness. We see this frequently in our work supporting organization redesign. The boxes of an organigram can be incredibly seductive. A redrawn organization chart can seem like an organizational problem neatly solved (and after all, we've done the relationships too; there are lines between the boxes, and sometimes dotted lines). However, often, not enough time has been spent having the type of conversations and dialogues that really open up some of the qualities of the existing relationships, and exploring what these relationships need to be in future if the organization design is to come to life. If we are constructing our organizational realities through the ways in which we participate and interact with one another (Gergen, 2009), then focusing only on our individual acts will not help us do this skilfully and intentionally. Without understanding and developing these relationships, we risk designing disparate notes, but not arriving at the chords and harmonic progressions we need to deliver our strategies.

The second thing that catches our ear in the Grove definition is this distinction between using the term harmony descriptively and prescriptively. Grove seems to accept that there are legitimate "precise" and "metaphorical" ways of working with the term, which we are delighted about. We could frame this as the difference between a musician's approach to music versus a musicologist's. In 2013 iRock Jazz held a series of interviews with jazz musicians and jazz experts to try and answer the question "what is jazz?" (The Great Jazz Debate, iRock Jazz, 2013). The experts all seemed to be striving for a definition, to be prescriptive about what is and isn't jazz. Their tendency was to focus on different defining elements or features of the musical form. The musicians on the other hand, seemed to be resisting definition. What they tended to speak to was the felt quality of the music, a description of the experience rather than a prescription of the ingredients. It is interesting that Grove allows room for both. Both approaches are potential routes to insight and learning and we are not interested in arguing which is "right or wrong". We would simply note that our dominant tendency in thinking about the world and organization is prescriptive, and holding ourselves open to playing with the qualitative, the felt, the metaphorical meanings of harmony may be worth experimenting with more too.

Variation: Harmony and sense making

In these Great Jazz Debate interviews the musicians spoke a lot from the frame of being in the middle of the soundscape of making jazz music. Their language is often about sensing, feeling, hearing, noticing, paying attention to what is going on in the moment. They seem to be operating from a world view that the information they need in order to navigate their way forward is present in the seeming chaos of the moment, and can be felt, heard, sensed if they can just tune in enough (they are not referring back to a definition of jazz and the elements they need to deliver to do it "properly"). We are put in mind again of Pythagoras and Johannes Kepler, with their idea of the harmony of the spheres as a metaphor for a natural and spiritual world that is deeply connected and patterned (deeply "organized"). And there seems to be a connection to what Snowden says is required of leaders in varying organizational contexts (Snowden, 2007). In a truly chaotic context, what is required is some kind of action. A chaotic system has no discernible order, and doing something and observing what happens is a way of beginning to sense into a situation. The act in itself provides something around which the situation can begin to coalesce, and we may move things from chaotic to complex. In a complex leadership context, we are still far from the world of plannable certainty. What is required here is paying exquisite attention to what is unfolding in the moment. What is the feel of the situation? How are people reacting and responding around me? Is there tension, anxiety, release? What are the harmonic undertones of my interactions? It seems to us that what Snowden is describing here is a leadership state similar to that of the "listening Mingus" we talked about in Chapter Four, with a presence, alertness and readiness to respond (Mingus, 1998). So, sensing into the harmony of a situation, even when that harmony may not initially be clear, may be a useful leadership experiment.

Variation: Choosing the key

However, mercifully, in organizational life we are not always parachuted into the middle of a jam session and asked to take a chorus. When musicians come to play together, they normally spend a bit of time agreeing on a context. In Western classical traditions this could be as detailed as agreeing the exact piece of music, and the exact bar number at which they will begin. In a jazz tradition, it may be an overall tune, and a particular harmonic key. In both cases, the musicians have enough of an agreed harmonic or tonal context to begin together. However, once they have begun, even in a classical tradition where the notes are written out, deep listening and responding to one another is vital if the music-making is to be successful.

And this idea of tonal organization is older and found much more widely than just in Western musical tradition. For example, the music of many cultures builds on the tonal platform of the drone. Grove defines this as:

A sustained droning sound, or a musical instrument or part of an instrument which produces such a sound and maintains it throughout a piece or section of music.

(Drone, *The Grove Dictionary of Music*, 2020)

This may be most familiar to many of us in the form of the Scottish bag pipe, and the held tonic and fifth notes which act as an anchor beneath the melody played on the chanter. So, in an organizational context, we might ask ourselves a number of questions around what our equivalent drones or harmonies are. What are the sustaining sounds that sit beneath everybody's melody lines? Or if we are joining a new organization or team, what is the harmonic undertone? Is it major or minor? What key are they playing in? How might I best join in harmoniously or otherwise? Alternatively, we could view setting the harmonic tone or key for the organization as a leadership task. As mentioned earlier, at the recording of *Kind of Blue,* Miles Davis (as band leader) arrived with scraps of paper outlining the modal scales he wanted the band to play within on each track. He literally "set the tone" for their work; not the full melody line, but he provided enough orientation to allow them to create and collaborate at their best.

And as well as playing effectively in the moment, another leadership task is often speaking to the organizational future. In her work on what makes organizations thrive (connected particularly with appreciative inquiry processes), Diana Whitney has explored deeply the power of helping groups create positive visions for the future (Cooperrider, D.; Whitney, D.; Stavros, J., 2008, pp. 3-7). From the perspective of positive psychology it can be enormously helpful for us to "paint pictures" of the destination we want to arrive at, working with the visual metaphor. However, it is also interesting that these visions of the future state are often significantly influenced by a powerful few. The challenge with a visual expression is, that once painted, it can be quite static. It can be difficult for others to find themselves in it, if they have not been part of the painting process. There is a risk that diverse viewpoints are excluded and the organizational future solidifies without them.

And we are also thinking now of the experience of paying attention to "what is" in organizational work ("us at our best"). If we ask groups these sorts of generative questions, when making sense of their current organizational contexts, people tend to work more widely with other senses, with feelings, intuitions. Here, Whitney also offers a build on the practice of working with the dominant visual metaphor, and wonders whether organizational "resonance" might not be a more generative way of articulating organizational "presents" and futures (Whitney, 2010). An organizational sound, future or present, involves all participants, in a way that painting the organizational picture might not.

Variation: Harmonic positions

If harmony is about the combination of notes, ideally resulting in the desired chords and harmonic progression, then it might be interesting to think about what position we play in our team or organizational harmony. Are we the person who always plays the tonic note, setting the foundation for the chord, and indicating with this gesture that others might want to fall in line with our suggestion? Or are we the person who jumps in swiftly with the major third when the tonic is played, following a strong lead and looking to help create a consonant harmonic sound? Alternatively, are we the person who always follows the tonic with a minor third, taking us in a harmonic direction that might be the equivalent of "we tried that last year and it didn't work"? We are playing with the metaphor here, but we would argue that in any healthy conversational culture, people are able to move around different harmonic positions, and play different roles in the chord voicings at different times. If you notice that you are always occupying the same position, it might be useful to check if this is always helpful. Am I playing a part in developing the harmony, or is the harmonic progression stuck or stagnant? In Barnett Pearce's work on the nature of dialogue and "coordinated management of meaning" (CMM) this might be referred to as an "unwanted repetitive pattern" (URP) (Pearce, 1989, p. 20). These are conversational positions we can find ourselves occupying frequently, particular in groups we spend a lot of time with (e.g. families or teams). The frequency with which we occupy a particular position can affect others' responses and expectations of the roles we are likely to play in any conversation, increasing the likelihood that we end up "stuck" in that position. Given the relational and organizational contexts we all work in are dynamic, any "stuck" responses are likely to be unhelpful in letting us thrive.

What this metaphor, and indeed good music, seems to be asking for, is healthy harmonic and musical development. And we can use this frame to think about our own harmonic development and growth as organizational participants. When learning the basics of harmony, it is often a breakthrough for fledgling musicians when they realise how much music they can make with three chords, I, IV and V – or C major, F major and G major in the key of C. This is the harmonic foundation of many popular and folk tunes, and also the gateway to the 12 bar blues. This is the point in their musical development where they can really begin to participate and play in groups, to work and communicate effectively with others. We might equate this with the early days of learning the ropes in our first jobs in organizations. There comes a point where we have enough competence to hold our own and work effectively with others. There are musicians who have made their careers working with these simple harmonic changes. However, there is also a whole new world of musical choices if we extend our harmonic knowledge and think about augmenting and substituting chords. A great example of this type of harmonic development is pianist and composer Thelonious Monk. He was known for extending the vocabulary of jazz music at the time through exploring alternative harmonic voicings. Even when playing a jazz standard with a widely known chord progression, Monk was able to find alternative harmonic routes through, which retained the essence of the tune, whilst somehow breathing new life into it. If we considered chords I, IV and V as entry level organizational competence, then Monk represents a path to finding our own unique style for working and leading. We may know how to run a department of 300 people, but how can we keep it fresh by finding alternative harmonic routes through? Guitar legend Jimi Hendrix reached a point where you could almost tell it was him by just hearing him play one chord, for example, E 7 with a sharpened 9th. This chord is at the core of a number of his hits such as *Purple Haze* and *Foxy Lady*. It contains both a major and a minor third, which gives it an ambiguous quality that can be tilted in either direction, hinting at major or minor keys. It allows for the major third common in country music, and the minor third common in blues. And the minor and major third played together offer a semitone dissonance which seems to speak to the zeitgeist of the late 60's. What might the equivalent of this harmonic uniqueness be for us in our participation in organizations?

Working in practice: Setting the harmonic tone

When working with leaders around their organizational challenges, we often find it helpful to think of harmony as the context in which they are operating. Artists are often very deliberate in creating the contexts in which they create. We're thinking of poet Dylan Thomas's writing shed on the cliffs of Laugharne in West Wales, a draughty outhouse littered with screwed up paper and empty beer bottles, and with the cry of the curlew audible from the mudflats below. Or the bright chaos of artist Francis Bacon's studio in Dublin, with paint pots of all colours stacked everywhere, and the floor padded with paper and old canvases. However unusual or even unappealing these may seem to us as places to work, they are deliberate choices that have a connection with the work that they produce. We notice that in organizations we are not often as deliberate about setting the context for our work. We tend to accept the situation we inherit when we join an organization, or are promoted to take over a team. Being more deliberate about setting the scene or choosing the key we are going to play in can be helpful.

We worked with a European police and fire network who were in the process of an organization transformation. Resourcing challenges, difficult working patterns, and changes in the types of services they needed to provide for the communities they supported, meant that they needed to be more agile, and collaborate across organizational boundaries. By nature, police and fire services tend to be very hierarchical, with orders flowing down through the ranks, and priorities often set (or reset) by the most senior leader in the room at the time. This type of culture can be helpful in supporting clarity of authority in emergency situations. However, there can be drawbacks such as reduced creativity and collaboration if only senior leadership voices are really heard.

At this time, the CEO was keen to get the wider teams together to outline the rationale for why they needed to make cultural and organizational changes, and to formally kick off the transformation program. Conscious of the importance of setting the harmonic tone, we chose not do this in the atrium of the organizational headquarters. This would have played into the organization's normal pattern of traditional hierarchical messages delivered from the organizational centre. It would also have emphasized a sense of "business as usual" which would have been unhelpful in garnering support for change. Instead, the event was moved to a nearby well-known blues venue, complete with dark wood panelling, cabaret tables, and a low stage for the band. The venue change got people interested in what was going on, and gave a sense that there really was something new about to happen here. On the day, instead of giving a stand-up keynote presentation on the transformation plans, the CEO sat on stage in a low chair and was interviewed about the organization, and about the challenges of shaping a context for people to create and collaborate. This shifted the conversational tone of the kick-off event from monologue, to dialogue, from receiving instruction to curiosity.

Amongst other things that came up in the interview was the challenge of not only getting people to contribute ideas across the whole organization, but to ensure that when they do they are heard. The conversation moved to an anecdote about The Rolling Stones. In the early 60's, rock'n'roll in the UK was cool and self-confident, and becoming a dominant force in youth culture. However, another musical genre that had been popular and was on the wane, was the British New Orleans jazz revival, championed by the likes of Chris Barber, Acker Bilk and Kenny Ball. These bands were characterized by their waistcoats, straw boaters, and beards, and the pervading sound of the banjo in the rhythm section; and by the time the Stones were on the rise they had become something of a figure of fun. The Stones had had some initial hits, but had reached a point where they were struggling for new ideas. Legend has it that one day, characteristically in a bar, guitarist Keith Richards got chatting with a banjo player, interested in chords and the different tunings of the banjo compared with the guitar. Mick Jagger was dismissive afterwards, joking "never listen to the banjo player". However, Richards ignored this and experimented with retuning his guitar to explore different voicings. What resulted from this initially was the riff for their next hit "Honky Tonk Women", and the harmonic seeds of more hits to come had been sown. For some reason this resonated deeply with the leadership teams of the police and fire networks. They identified the banjo player with the smaller voices in the organization that were being dismissed (recognizing that many roles in different ways could be seen as "banjo players"), and realized that these voices might just hold the disruptive information that the organization needed to evolve and innovate. "Always listen to the banjo player" became a key phrase that they came back to throughout the transformation, almost a musical *Leitmotif* that reminded them of the spirit and importance of what it was that they'd set out to do together (we believe there were even T-shirts printed!). And there was something about the context of that first meeting that helped them listen in a different way; and indeed, in hindsight, many people we spoke to said they knew that this was going to be different from the moment they got the invitation to the blues club. There seems to be something helpful for people about setting the tone for work to be done together, in choosing an appropriate key, outlining the harmonic context. It may take time up front but it often pays off.

Working in practice: Creating space for harmonic relationships between notes

A colleague of ours was engaged in a digital transformation programme for a global engineering business. This was a major initiative involving the migration of several large  IT systems, and the development of a number of new platforms. The senior leadership were well aware of the significance of the undertaking, and of how much was riding on it.

They made resource available to ensure the smooth running of the project. Amongst other things, teams of business architects were deployed to map requirements in detail and be certain that all processes in the organization were captured and taken into account. They spent significant time in each functional area understanding how they worked and needed to work, and the systems were designed accordingly. The language of architecture, blue-printing, detailed specification dominated conversations. However, when the system prototype designs began to emerge, a small number of the team began to notice that the design was so tight it left little room for collaboration, or innovation. An understandable anxiety about getting the project "right" had driven the business architects to focus on all the individual notes of the score, all the functional tasks and pieces of data that needed homes. What they had not designed for was the harmonic context, the relationships between the notes. What was helpful here was introducing a new frame or set of principles for design, those that borrowed from the pre-conditions for good music making or improvisation. Engineers from across the businesses needed to be able to "hear what each other were playing". There needed to be enough flexibility to allow for serendipity, for people to develop themes they hear from others, or notice when the key of what they are playing has changed. The musical metaphor, alongside the metaphor of architectural design, helped ensure that what was implemented was not only thought through and planned in detail, but also had the flexibility to allow for the relationships across the organization, and for changing harmonic contexts.

Working in practice: Listening for harmonic nuance

When we're engaged in organizational change work we're keen to understand the context the business is in, and the reason for the changes needed. For example, we may  hear that there has been disruption in an organization's marketplace, and that it needs to change its way of doing business to remain competitive. There is usually a dominant version of this story that we get from groups at the heart of the change, for example transformation teams charged with "steering" major changes. However, what we have noticed is that, if we listen carefully to how individuals talk about the changes, there are often nuances and differences which can be worth catching. If we think of the metaphor of harmonic mood, each individual brings their own harmonic mood to an organizational change situation. This may be coloured by previous experiences, by personality preferences, and may shift from day to day. And the harmonic mood has an influence on how we play and act into the organization.

So, in the above example of disruption in a marketplace, we may hear one individual talk about the need to "evolve" the way they do business, to grow new opportunities in adjacent fields; to cultivate new ways of working together. The language here is suggestive of the natural world, it is a change that is gradual but comes to fruition over time. It speaks to nurturing and feeding an organization and trusting that things will ripen and the harvest will come.

Equally, we may hear another individual talking about new competition disrupting the market as having created "a burning platform". We are now metaphorically perhaps on an oil rig with flames licking at the pilings. The change probably needs to be quick, if not instant. And the consequences of the choices we make will be swiftly felt. We hope you can hear that the harmonic mood that each of these individuals brings to the change programme is likely to be quite different. Lakoff and Johnson in their work in this field see metaphor as "pervasive in everyday life, not just in language but in thought and action". They argue that these linguistic concepts "structure what we perceive, how we get around in the world, and how we relate to other people" (Lakoff & Johnson, 2003, p. 3). And this is exactly what we have experienced in organizations. If people are operating from different underpinning metaphors about the transformation work in hand, and operating from different harmonic moods, then the way they lead and act in to the change will be different. A burning platform metaphor speaks to acting swiftly, at pace, with fear and anxiety as the fuel for change. The evolution metaphor speaks to a more measured, calmer way of leading, looking to nourish the organization, trusting in time that the efforts in the garden will bear fruit. We have used an extreme contrast here, but in our experience, and in practitioner research into transformation, there are very often differing metaphors at play in the minds of those leading change (Metalogue, 2018). Listening out for these, surfacing them, and discussing them as a group can really help leadership teams act together into the change they want to bring about with a more consistent approach; playing in the same key.

Working in practice: Training the ear

It's not a new idea that listening in leadership and organizational life is an important skill, even if it is something we still observe many people struggling with given the pace 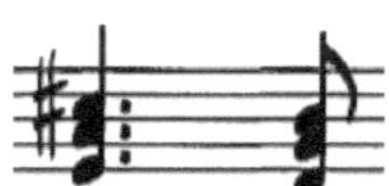 of change we face. And even where we do experience good listening, it is often listening of a particular kind. We seem to be conditioned (by our education and socialization in organizations) to listen at the level of individual notes in conversations, facts, figures, actions. This phenomenon has its roots in the dominant scientific paradigm of the last several hundred years which seeks to isolate "problems" into their constituent parts in order to understand and solve them. This is a helpful but partial approach, and if it is the only way in which we listen, then we often miss hearing the underlying harmonies and nuances of the relationships between the notes, figures, or actions. When working with teams we often find it helpful to get them to practice listening at different levels. For example, we might ask individual members to focus solely on listening to the emotions behind what someone is saying; forgetting the facts and figures, and just reporting back what they are hearing on an emotional level. Is the person excited by what they are conveying? Do they sound hesitant, or bored? Is there a moment where they sound anxious? What does the sound, volume, or pace of their voice say? What words or metaphors do they choose that might reveal what is going on emotionally? Is the dominant vocabulary of the conversation positive or negative?

Hearing this level of data can allow us to reflect on what might be happening beneath the surface layer of the individual notes being played. People typically find this difficult, and they seem to automatically start by scribbling down some of the facts and actions. However, with time this muscle develops. And what can be particularly powerful is exploring any hunches or hypotheses that you develop from listening at the emotional level with the individuals afterwards. This can result in a conversation of a different kind to the one we would normally have "about" the subject in question, and often deepens and develops relationships.

Working in practice: Creating harmonic space

We spoke earlier about the choice of the blues venue being helpful in signalling that it was ok for the group to have a different type of conversation together (in Working in practice: Setting the harmonic tone). And, indeed, many organizations are becoming sensitive to how physical space affects the way dialogue and relationships flow. A famous example is the Crick Institute in London which was designed to "bring together 1,500 of Europe's brightest minds from six different organizations to solve the world's most vexing scientific problems" (HOK, 2020). The design emphasizes communal spaces to allow for serendipitous conversations across the six different organizations, knowing that this type of "cross-fertilization" is at the heart of innovation. The physical space nudges the type of conversations that are desired.

In a less monolithic way, it is possible to work more deliberately with sound to shape a tonal environment conducive to the way people need to work together. We worked on a large-scale leadership development programme for aspiring leaders in a national administrative system. The programme brought leaders together from across the organization, and getting to know each other and building networks was an important objective of the programme. One particular three-day module saw them go through an intense experiential simulation, and then a series of reflective processes to help them examine and learn from their experiences. On the morning of day one, the harmonic / tonal space we wanted was one of conversation and connection. As people arrived, having not seen each other for a while, we actively greeted participants, re-introducing them to one another, and the tone which developed was warm, convivial, and spoke to renewing and deepening acquaintances. The groups knew there was a degree of uncertainty attached to this module, so it was helpful for them on day one to be met with a harmonic mood which spoke to connection, talking to people known to them, and fostering a group environment that felt safe enough to take risks in. Day two was the morning of the simulation. The groups had to be in the room at 08:30 sharp for an unknown appointment. The tone we wanted for day two was focussed, with enough helpful nerves to ensure people were at their best. When participants arrived we either did not greet them, or did so in a subdued fashion. The room was quiet and remained so. We busied ourselves with silent preparation activities, leaving the group to their own devices. An expectant hush was the tonal cue for what was to come. Day two for most people was a fairly full-on experience. Yet from a learning design perspective the reflection on, and inquiry into day two's experiences was where the real insights and learning were likely to come. So, on day three when participants arrived, we set the tone in the room with medium slow-paced music, often Miles Davis's *Kind of Blue.* As mentioned earlier, the modal nature of the harmonies here means that the tracks do not rush through chord changes to obvious conclusions. The music explores slowly, dwells in introspection, congruent with the nature of the day's reflective learning. And given that participants had often had very different experiences the day before, having soft music in the room meant that those who wanted to sit quietly and process were able to, and those who felt like talking to others could do that too. It was a harmonic environment that picked them up where each of them were, and allowed us all to move forward together into the day. These may seem like incidental choices, but over multiple cohorts we noticed how significantly the "sound" in the room at the start of each day framed how people engaged.

And tonal interventions can be even less elaborate than that. Many facilitators work with a Tibetan singing bowl or equivalent to help them create holding environments. At the start of a team conversation, for example, striking the singing bowl produces a sustained resonant gong sound. It draws the ear and focuses everyone's attention on the central point from which the sound is emitting, but also lets the ear travel with the resonances around the room. It is a sound which encourages a centering in of focus, and also a settling in to space. By heightening the aural sense, it can also be helpful in setting the expectation that we are moving into a conversational space where listening and letting others' thoughts resonate is what is required. When working without the singing bowl, it is noticeable that the conversation that starts is often pacier and sometimes a little ragged; it requires more holding and settling by the facilitator. When the singing bowl is used, on the other hand, the conversations tend to start more slowly and smoothly, at a pace that the group can sustain.

And even when we are working on our own, experimenting with being deliberate about the tonal space we create for ourselves can be helpful. One visual artist we know painted through many an Amsterdam night in his studio with Nick Cave's "Babe I'm on Fire" on loop. For him it was this music that triggered the painting and the visual expression, and provided a harmonic container which allowed him go on a journey with the paint. Sound can unlock as well as contain, and we'd encourage you to experiment with it in organizational contexts.

Concluding thoughts: Towards harmonic savvy
We've noted a tendency in our organizational thoughts and actions to pay attention to individual notes, and miss the connections between them; the harmonic context that they

create. And it is not enough just to pay attention to the connections between the notes we are playing individually, to our own harmonic mood. If we are to work successfully together, we need to explore the wider harmonies in the organization and come to some agreement. Whilst this is complex, we exist in harmonic relationship with one another whether we like it or not, and if we are not to be unintentionally and unhelpfully discordant, then developing an ear for nuance and harmony is an important skill. If we are "tone deaf" to what is going on, then we are likely to make interventions that baffle and confuse others, or send messages that run completely counter to what we intend.

It speaks to the sensing and intuiting that Snowden sees as so important in complexity leadership (Snowden, 2007). It is also the savvy that Parzival develops over many hard years out in the forests. At his first visit to the Grail Castle, he is so unaware of the context in which he finds himself, that his actions are discordant in the extreme and send the whole world back into suffering and chaos. When he arrives the second time, his harmonic ear is tuned in acutely to the depths and resonances of the experience that is unfolding before him. He is able to say the only right thing for that moment; like Naná Vasconcelos's bell playing, it needn't be much, but at the right time it can really count.

7

Rhythm

You might like to read this while listening to:

Song For My Father, Horace Silver

Theme

Our old friend Grove seems to be less certain on this one and cross-references a number of secondary sources in what is quite a long entry on rhythm. The abridged definition that we found interesting reads:

Generically, a 'movement marked by the regulated succession of strong or weak elements' (Oxford English Dictionary). In etymological discussions of the term there is a tension between rhythm as continuously 'flowing' and rhythm as periodically punctuated movement......Rhythm and pitch are the two primary parameters of musical structure (Meyer, E 1973). For in specifying the tonal and rhythmic organization of a work we believe we have captured its essential structure. Changes in instrumentation, orchestration or dynamics (i.e. changes to the secondary parameters) are understood as different arrangements of the same musical work, whereas alterations in pitch or rhythm may result in a new or different work.

(Rhythm, *The Grove Dictionary of Music*, 2020)

What strikes us first here is the paradoxical quality that Grove attributes to rhythm. It seems to have quantum properties and somehow manage to be wave and particle at the same time. If we think of flowing rhythm in terms of organization, this might equate to the day to day routines of a "normal" week. It might be the gentle patterns of coffee breaks, informal conversations over lunch, the colleagues we normally meet, the morning rituals of opening up laptops, starting up systems. These may even be rhythmic elements we barely notice, that just carry us along from one moment to the next. And in its most useful manifestation we are thinking of Csikszentmihalyi's work on flow. He defines flow as "a state in which people are so involved in an activity that nothing else seems to matter; the experience is so enjoyable that people will continue to do it even at great cost, for the sheer sake of doing it" (Csikszentmihalyi, 1990, p.4). This is a mode which has great potential for creativity and productivity, as well as being a pleasurable experience for those involved. How might we try and shape flowing rhythms in our organizations that supported these states more often? However, Csikszentmihalyi also draws our attention to a potential shadow side to flowing rhythm. Once in the flow, people may be carried along with it even "at great cost". Perhaps if we are in certain types of flow for too long we may not realize that we are stuck in an unhelpful pattern. At an organizational level this might be a tried and tested organizational practice or process that is repeated long after newer or more efficient ways of working become available. If it is known and trusted, and we are skilled at carrying it out, maybe we have a vested interest in staying in this old flow, even "at great cost" to our competitive edge as an organization.

Again, we are put in mind of the coordinated management of meaning, and the idea of "unwanted repetitive patterns" (Pearce, 1989, p. 20). The term "unwanted" leaves the door open for the idea of "wanted" patterns. If we can find ways of reflecting on our flowing rhythms periodically, and asking ourselves whether the flow is helping us, then perhaps we move to the realm of "wanted repetitive patterns". The "groove" can be helpful, but how might we design for deliberate flowing rhythmic elements, and guard against those that would lull us to sleep when disruption comes?

And perhaps this speaks to the other quality Grove assigns to rhythm, that of "punctuation". To us, punctuation suggests a quality of rhythm that draws attention to itself. Audible drum beats, or a crash on a cymbal that momentarily pull us out of flow and ask us to notice something afresh. In organizational terms these might be annual or quarterly strategy planning or review cycles, quarterly town hall meetings, team away days, extraordinary meetings around major events. These might be occasions when we are pulled out of day to day flows and given the opportunity, or asked, to pay attention to what we are doing organizationally at a different rhythmic level. If these become too regular in themselves, then they too can slip into a type of flow. However, if we can hold onto this principle of punctuation and awakening when designing these rhythmic moments, they might help us guard against unhelpful flow. And we've seen this at work in recent times in national responses to the COVID-19 pandemic. Multiple governments introduced punctuating rhythms early on in the form of daily briefings. They varied from country to country but most were quickly imbued with a sense of ritual and import. They were designed to help punctuate anxiety, fear, emotion, the tide of media reporting around the unfolding pandemic, with a moment of official clarity. How effective this was, or how pure the intents of respective governments around "clarity" were, we suspect will be the stuff of inquiries for some years to come. Nevertheless, it strikes us as a useful example of deliberate use of a punctuating rhythm.

Variation: A fundamental quality

Another thing that caught our attention in the Grove entry is how it names rhythm (and pitch) as being fundamental to defining the quality of "a work". Changing which instrument plays a particular melodic line, or altering the volume or emphasis of certain notes, on the other hand, is seen to be merely variation or embellishment within the same piece. Playing with the metaphor in organizational terms, how significant might rhythm be in defining "work" (as it is in defining "a musical work")? Perhaps if we are in the world of organizational change, altering which instrument plays a line might be the equivalent of moving a task or process from one person or department to another. It doesn't fundamentally change the "work" but there might be a noticeable change in the character of how the "work" is carried out. This might be the world of process optimization, drives for efficiency through making tweaks and changes within the existing organizational frame. So, in this vein, changes to rhythm (or pitch) mean we are changing "the work"; and perhaps here we are in the world of organization transformation; major shifts in the operations and nature of "the work" being done, the music being played. And organizational transformation being a term we hear a lot, perhaps this is a way of checking what we are all talking about when we use it. When we frame our changes, is it instrumentation (or tweaks and efficiencies) we are talking about; or are we really looking at major changes to our organizational rhythm (transformation)?

And we are conscious that by comparison organizational transformation is starting to sound overwhelming and monolithic. However, we might take solace in learnings from complexity science here, which show that small changes can have ripple effects which spread widely across large systems. It is possible to "transform" large systems by starting with small acts; however, the caveat, based on what we have just been exploring here, might be that these small acts need to be at the level of rhythm or pitch, not just instrumentation or dynamics. A musical example of fundamental change through addressing a rhythmic element of organization is Steve Reich's *Clapping Music* (1972). Written for at least two performers this sees one performer clap a 12/8 rhythm. The other joins in but every 8 to 12 bars shifts the rhythm by one eighth note. Eventually the piece ends up with a unison rhythm being clapped again, but not before it has provided us with a live example of the organizational variety that is available through small shifts at a rhythmic level.

Variation: Rhythm and the embodied in organization

Reich's piece is a literal example of using the body to create rhythm. And this makes us think of the role of rhythm and the embodied in organizations. If we are in the office early (pandemics permitting), we might notice the relative quiet at first; and then as 9am approaches, the noise of people arriving (with their bodies); the patterning of footfall in the corridors; doors being opened or closed, bags landing on desks to be unpacked for the day. We've noted the risk earlier of our metaphors slipping, and have given ourselves the permission to go with it; so it's worth pointing out the links here between organization and choreography. Choreography combines the visual aspect with the rhythmic, but as a metaphor gives us a way into what it feels like to be in the midst of the rhythms and movements of an organization. When Shaw talked about organization as "ensemble improvisation" (Shaw, 2002, p. 96) our initial connection was with musical improvisation. We remember now that she also trained as a dancer, and we might very well think of organizational (consulting) work as akin to being engaged in a dance. Indeed, Bateson quotes the great American dancer, Isadora Duncan, in *Steps to an Ecology of Mind* (Bateson, 1972, p. 137):

"If I could tell you what it meant, there would be no point in dancing it"

Bateson uses this to highlight what he sees as an epistemological flaw in Western scientific practices, which operate from the assumption that, with enough analysis, all can be defined and articulated. The point of dance is in the dancing, and speaks to ways of knowing that are about the embodied experience and can't always be captured on paper.

And the embodied experience is often ignored in organization too. We looked earlier at Stacey's ideas of organizations as complex responsive processes (Stacey, 2003), where "organizations" are a pattern of interaction, of gestures and responses between organizational participants. This, combined with our abilities to enable and constrain each other's intentions (e.g. through hierarchical power), leads to the rich and often unpredictable experience that is organizational life. Our primary gestures and responses in organization are perhaps verbal, yielding the idea of organizations as audible dialogic improvisation. However, our embodied experience can play into this game of enabling and constraint too. For example, improvisational theatre director Keith Johnstone talks about how we are always reading verbal and non-verbal status relationships in organizations, and changing our behaviours and what we say and don't say accordingly (Johnstone, 1981). He refers to this as a "kinetic dance" as we negotiate physical cues that suggest others are higher or lower status than us in any given moment, (i.e. a potential threat to us or not) or someone we may be able to dominate to our advantage (e.g. food in evolutionary terms) (Johnstone, 1999, p. 232). Similarly, theatre director Patsy Rodenburg uses the embodied experience of being "in organization" with people to reflect on how we choose to interact (Rodenburg, 2008). She thinks of three circles of energy that characterize our actions. In Circle 1 we are more turned in on ourselves, quietly spoken, perhaps with less eye contact; it is an energy often triggered by a sense of threat or intimidation in a situation. However, it is a mode where we are concerned with ourselves and not really in contact with what is going on, and not in a good position to respond well. In Circle 3 our energy is high and pushed outwards. This may be the result of confidence, but could just as easily be bravado with a sense of anxiety at its heart. Once more we are not in touch with what is going on. Circle 2 energy is more balanced, and centred. We are in a state where we are holding onto our confidence enough, but are also connected with the situation at hand, and sensing and responding in the moment. This is the best state for responsive acting on stage. And based on what we have been exploring seems to be analogous with what many have claimed as the ideal state for disciplines as varied as dancing, musical improvisation, and even leading in complex organizational contexts.

This level of interconnection would seem to support

Grove's claims for the fundamental importance of rhythm. It seems to have a deep human significance. We think now of American dancer Gabrielle Roth's therapeutic work with her 5 rhythms approach (Roth, 2004). Groups are led through 5 stages of dance accompanied by heavily percussive rhythms as a way of tuning into and working through various psychological and emotional barriers and stucknesses. And the fundamental nature of rhythm and dance is something philosopher Alan Watts would appear to agree with in this memorable appeal to reason in a lecture on metaphysics:

"We thought of life by analogy with a journey, a pilgrimage, which had a serious purpose at the end .....But we missed the point the whole way along. It was a musical thing and you were supposed to sing or to dance while the music was being played."   (Watts, 2018)

We encounter the metaphor of the journey in organizations all the time. It is linked to the idea of "targets" and "visions", and the reassuring processions of quarterly metrics that track the journey and are standard business practice. And Watts' point is a stark reminder that life and organization is essentially participative, and if we fail to feel the rhythms and dance the dance along the way, then we are missing out.

Variation: The sound of silence
Along with the punctuation points of the cymbal crash, another key aspect that defines rhythm is the pauses and silences in between. Without these it would all just be (un-

helpful) noise and our rhythms would not make sense. In organizational terms we might equate silences with organizational pauses, perhaps holidays or periods of rest, seasons which are quieter in the organization's year. Rather than become anxious about filling these "slow seasons" or periods of "down-time" with activity, perhaps we might be able to recognize that silence and pause are a fundamental part of rhythm, and play a vital role. In organizational consulting, working actively to hold silences and pauses in a group conversation, for example, can sometimes allow the space for something necessary to be said. The silence can be the break in the rhythm that a team needs in order to hear itself anew, and name a difficult dynamic. And in a medical context we think of the surgical timeout, described as "an immediate pause by the entire surgical team to confirm the correct patient, procedure, and site". This was introduced by US Medical Commissions to design in a pause in the busyness, data and status play of the operating room, a flowing rhythm that could otherwise result in mistakes being made if not checked (Pelligrini, 2017).

And we think of the major period of pause that many of us have found ourselves in through the COVID-19 global pandemic. One colleague referred to this rather beautifully as "the grand fermata". Grove defines a fermata as:

The sign of the corona or point surmounted by a semicircle showing the end of a phrase or indicating the prolongation of a note or a rest beyond its usual value.
(Fermata, *The Grove Dictionary of Music*, 2020)

We didn't expect to read the word "corona" there. And we wonder if there are things to be learned if, in our organizations, we hold some of our silences for longer than we habitually do.

Working in practice: Designing for breaks in the rhythm

We worked with a manufacturing company which had been successful in rapidly growing its business. The result was a need  for more and more efficiency out of its production facilities, particularly in the short to medium term whilst it planned to bring more production capacity online. The rhythm of the business was already fast flowing and was increasing in pace as the order books filled. Operators complained that the pace was starting to feel relentless. As the pressure increased, occasional mistakes were creeping in and the quality governance key performance indicators, whilst not alarming, were starting to move in the wrong direction. At this point, it also became apparent that the new production capacities would be delayed. It was a time when instincts and anxiety suggested that what everyone needed to do was run faster. However, the organization realized that levels of resilience in the team were dropping, and that this simply wasn't sustainable. Examined through the metaphor of rhythm, it became apparent that the organizational rhythm was about to tip into becoming (unhelpful) noise. The pauses between the percussive elements were being squeezed out. As errors increased, the anxiety about not having time to make mistakes also increased, which was starting to close down opportunities for learning and error prevention. Upon reflection, what the operations team decided to do was design pauses back into the working day. Counter-intuitively they shortened shifts to allow ring-fenced time at shift-end to review, log and learn from things that had come up over the course of the shift. This meant people were able to share and explore challenges in a context which wasn't about snatched conversations with a supervisor in the "heat of battle". Over time, staff also reported that these designed pauses allowed them time to connect and also decompress together at the end of the shift. Over a number of weeks, they observed that they were feeling better able to cope with the strain of the situation. Engagement saw a slight increase, and the quality indicators also improved. We wonder about the connection between "silence" and "resilience". Etymologically they have different roots, so perhaps it is at best an "eye rhyme" (to mix our metaphors again). Silence goes back to "silere" or "to be quiet and still". Resilience to "salire", "to jump or leap" back ("re"). Yet even "silere" and "salire" seem close enough as sounds to suggest some connection. They seem to speak to some relationship, where the practice of being silent might contribute to the ability to leap. Could "silere" be the pause to "salire"s percussive rhythmic element? It seems to fit with our experience that moments of pause and reflection have enormous benefits in terms of increasing resilience.

And we have seen this in our and others' work with healthcare systems too. As frontline healthcare systems around the world came under extreme pressure as the first COVID-19 waves hit, staff reported leaving long shifts exhausted, and struggling to process the stress and strain of what they had been witnessing. To compound this, many workers were choosing to stay away from home, particularly if they had vulnerable family members, for fear of spreading infection. This meant they were often returning exhausted to isolated quarters to refuel and sleep before going back to work. And depending on shift patterns, these periods of rest were often at times of the day and night when it was not easy to get in touch with family and friends to decompress. In response to this some healthcare systems began making online "drop in" spaces available on virtual platforms. These were places of pause, where staff could log in to connect, either in small groups or one to one, with colleagues or coaches; places to start to make sense of things together, or even just to let off steam. These weren't mandatory sessions, simply a "designed pause" outside of the relentless rhythm of the emergency response, which some found hugely helpful.

At other times, we've found it helpful to design breaks to help organizations reconnect with their own rhythms. We worked with a client in the energy sector whose senior leadership team was having difficulties developing its working practices and relationships. The team were spread across a number of different geographies, and all held specialist briefs for different aspects of the energy company's sales and operations. Whilst they had been meeting regularly in an effort to grow together, they still felt like a group of individuals, not a cohesive team. When they came together they informed the others of what was going on in their areas, but, outside of this, reported feeling isolated and unconnected to what was going on elsewhere. One musical exercise that helped them get a sense of what they were aiming for in their team development is something we call "The Fade". As a group we develop a rhythmic pattern through clapping, vocal percussive noises, or even using percussion instruments if they are at hand. We get the rhythm good and loud, and the more the rhythm swings, the better. Once we have a sense that the whole team know the rhythm and have found their way in, then we start to play with the dynamics. First louder, then quieter. Over time the team gets better and better at calibrating the dynamics as we bring them up and down, whilst maintaining the rhythm. We then work towards bringing the rhythm down to silence, and then asking the team to bring the rhythm back in on a sign from us. This sometimes takes a few attempts, but eventually the teams learn to sense the rhythm even if it is not audible, and remain in sync with each other. For this dispersed team, it became a helpful experience of staying rhythmically connected and aligned whilst not "hearing from each other". That "inner ear" for the team's rhythm, its underlying "groove", became the heart of what they wanted to develop together; a sort of "metaphorical outcome" for the series of team development sessions we ran.

Working in practice: Finding the perfect rhythm?

We often work with leaders who are extremely dedicated to developing their leadership experience and expertise, to supporting their teams well, and to getting their business operations set up perfectly to pave the way for everyone's success. The sense of responsibility and work ethic is admirable; and sometimes we notice that it brings a bit of pressure and strain with it, and that the leaders in question aren't always having much fun.

It puts us in mind of the heady days of the birth of synthesized drum machines. At the Frankfurter Musikmesse at some point in the early 80's one of us stumbled on a booth displaying a drum machine which would give you the perfect rhythm with "no mistakes". No longer would the pain of fallible human drummers rushing or dragging the beat need to be felt. The early adopter end of the music industry was sold, and the first hits with "perfect rhythms" made their way out of the record presses and onto the dance floors of Europe.

A few years later, drum machines were being seen more and more widely. Back at the Frankfurter Musikmesse we were intrigued to see the latest developments. The star product of the show this time was a synthesizer with a specially developed button called "the human factor". Our inner geek got the better of us, and we dove into the manual and realized that at its core the "human factor" feature relied on a random error generator in the reproduction of the rhythms. Once the initial novelty of perfect drum beats had worn off, artists and listeners alike had noticed that there was something missing, something cold or even suspect, and the technicians had responded by designing it back in.

When working with leaders who are feeling the burden of responsibility, or a drive to perfection, this little anecdote often helps free up the space for not having everything "nailed down", for allowing a little more human fallibility in. And an experimental frame for leadership practice, rather than a frame that suggests carrying out a set of procedures perfectly, can be helpful, particularly where contexts are uncertain, or innovative approaches are needed. As Miles Davis is often quoted as saying, in these contexts in particular, "if you're not making a mistake, that's a mistake".

With other leaders we've looked at varying their leadership style through the metaphor of rhythm. We sometimes start by looking at their job or role description, or perhaps the strategy for their department. This is what is expected of them on paper. It could be seen as the time signature of the piece, that says the organization expects them to be playing in 4/4 time. The standard approach to 4/4 time is emphasizing each beat on the beat **1**, 2, 3, 4; **2**, 2, 3, 4; **3**, 2, 3, 4 and so on. Keeping that beat requires competence, and it'll take you places; but it lacks a little style and interest. If you are in a leadership role where what is needed is more than carrying out your defined role competently; if you need to connect and build relationships, inspire and motivate your team, then doing something a bit more with the rhythm can be helpful.

For example, we could leave some of the beats out: X, 2, 3, 4; X, 2, 3, 4. That shifts things. Or leave even more out: X, 2, X, 4; X, 2, X, 4. Or even start adding things in, emphasizing off beats. Here we are moving to syncopated rhythms whilst never having left the "leadership brief" of the 4/4 time signature. So, in a coaching context for example, it can be fruitful to explore what "syncopated leadership" might look like for the leader in question. What beats could they leave out? Are there habits they have that they could experiment with suppressing, in order to see how the team respond to the different rhythm? Are there beats in the bar that they habitually play, that they could get others to play; is there some letting go of control of certain tasks that is worth experimenting with? Or what might be the equivalent of the surprising off-beat hi-hat? Are there things that they have not shared with their team about themselves that might be an enriching addition to the rhythm? Could risking sharing something "off-beat" help relationships develop to a level beyond the competent, professional, and "on time"? If we think of leading and participating in organization as being part of a dance, how might we dance it with more panache?

Working in practice: Rhythm and comping

In jazz combos, piano, drums, bass or guitar often make up what is known as the rhythm section. Part of their role is to pro-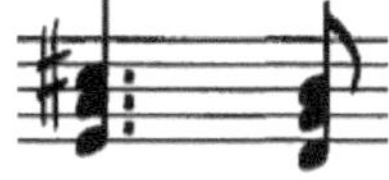

vide the rhythmic bedrock for the music making, and to accompany or "comp" the solo instruments or singers. As jazz styles evolved, rhythm section instrumentalists also featured as soloists, and the spirit of "comping" became something that applied to all musicians playing. The moment you are not soloing, your role is to support your colleagues well and make them look good. In improvisational theatre Keith Johnstone refers to this principle as the "yes, and..." principle (Johnstone, 1981). For a successful improvisation to develop, players must take an idea or suggestion given by their colleague, accept it (say yes) and build on it. The alternative, which Johnstone notes seeing a lot in organizations and educational institutions is "yes, but...". He terms this a "block", as it halts the energy of the other person's suggestion, and moves towards either rejecting it, or offering an alternative. "Yes, and.." is a mentality that invites unexpected information (offers) and operates from the assumption that there is merit in them, and that something can be done with them. "Yes, but.." is a mentality which operates from the assumption that something already known to me is better than what you have suggested.

We see these patterns in organizations we work with too. Sometimes, the "yes, but..." can be the voice of experience which is the guiding hand offering a course correction. However, more often than not, we see the "yes, but..." tendency becoming problematic as conversational cultures emerge where it is difficult to get agreement to move forward. A model we often connect with these dynamics is David Kantor's Four

Player model (Kantor, 2012). Through his work in family therapy he identified four common roles people occupy at different times in group conversations. Someone might make a "move", for example, coming up with a suggestion or proposal. Another might choose to "follow" and support the move (an equivalent to "yes, and...", particularly if the move is further developed). A third may choose to "oppose" the "move" (a possible "yes, but..." or block). And finally, a fourth person may "bystand or observe", perhaps coming up with a reframing of the situation, or a comment on process at a different level. Typically, we occupy all of these positions at different times, and all types of position can be helpful. However, what can happen with family groups or teams is that they become stuck in patterns of interaction that start to get in the way of what they are trying to do.

For example, we worked with a team from a technical engineering firm who were keen to develop their ways of working with one another. The group was struggling to make decisions. In terms of the Four Player model we observed that when someone made a "move", what happened next was another "move", or a "bystanding" intervention. Rather than building on a "move" made with a "follow", others made their own "moves", contributing their own ideas, without having really seemed to have heard or acknowledged the initial suggestion. When a "move" was followed by a "bystand" this was often in the form of a reframe, which served to neutralize the original "move" by suggesting an alternative perspective from which to explore the question in hand, or indeed suggesting a new question. With limited "following" moves, it had become difficult for the group to progress ideas. And where things did move forward, often they would grind to a halt later on as there had been "oppose" sentiments in the group but they had not found voice at the time.

Using the Four Player Model to identify and call out some of their stuck patterns, became a way of hearing afresh what was going on; and even allowed some humor in as the team caught themselves at it. In addition, the jazz metaphor and the ethos of "comping" was a helpful way of speaking to what they were aiming for in terms of their culture of support for one another. With this as the bedrock, we facilitated a series of team meetings developing the idea of their responding using a "yes, and.." rather than "yes, but..." frame. It's a simple frame, and not a new idea. However, over time, the team reported that their conversations were less stuck and blocked. It was motivating for them to see ideas move forward with momentum and backing. And some team members even spoke to feeling able to offer riskier, and less "thought through" ideas; with the sense that this was helping them, as a team, come up with more creative solutions.

Working in practice: Learning to hear polyrhythms

In thinking about organizational rhythm it would be easy to assume that the ideal, although perhaps unachievable, would be a steady 4 / 4. 4 / 4 seems more stable than the fluid 3 /4 waltz time. It is the basis of many a piece of 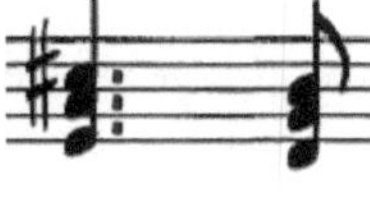

march music, with its links to ideas of a well aligned organization where people are "in step" with one another. However, when working with organizations to think about how they deal with disruptions, we often find the cybernetic idea of "ultra-stability" helpful (Ashby, 1952, pp. 80-99). In Ashby's terms, our desired 4 / 4 beat is a simple system. Its logic is intrinsic. It is not hooked into information from the outside world, and as such, whilst it may sound solid, it is susceptible to unexpected disruption. An "ultra-stable system" on the other hand is in constant communication with its environment. Rather than focusing on its own solid beat, it is looking for rhythmic disturbance and disruption in its environment, in order to adapt and respond to it. As a result, it is able to provide a dynamic stability that remains stable as its environment changes. It is the equivalent of the drummer in communication with the musicians around them, responding to suggestions the tempo needs changing, as opposed to our 1980s drum machine sticking to the metrically perfect rhythm.

We worked with a start-up tech business which had just reached a size where it was beginning to feel more mature. After a number of exciting and risky years, the founding partners were delighted to have reached a more stable level of operation. They were tired from the journey, and at a deep personal level were yearning for a period where they could more steadily grow and develop their "baby". They knew the world of start-ups was volatile, but now, having made it work, the simple stability of that 4 / 4 rhythm was very appealing. Working with the idea of "ultra-stable systems" they were able to recognize that, whilst they might achieve the seemingly stable 4 / 4 for a time, ultimately it was a more vulnerable organizational rhythm for them. They were able to set up small teams whose role it was to scan their markets for disturbance, and also to question and try and disrupt their business model from within. Rather than hoping that the disruptive years were gone, by actively accepting that they needed to look for and respond to disruption to be more stable, they were able to set their "baby" on a more robust path.

And we think of this in the context of leadership development too. When we are walking in a steady 4/4 rhythm we are using muscle groups familiar to us and we feel stable. However, if we really want to strengthen our core muscles, then we need to expose our body to less expected movements, to the occasional off-beat or syncopation in order to activate muscles we don't normally use. Indeed, much high intensity physical training exposes the body to eccentric movements, to teach it to remain strong and stable even in the midst of disruption. Clearly this needs to be treated with caution, as too much strain will lead to injury. However, finding the edge which has the training benefit is the key. As leaders, listening to our teams and organizations, we can tune our ear to the steady 4 / 4 of our usual rhythms. This will probably feel familiar and comfortable for us. However, in any organization there will be cross-rhythms, poly-rhythms, patterns that run counter to what we hear, or would like to hear. To find our training edge it is worth listening out for the rhythms that seem to disrupt the simple organizational life, and finding ways of exploring them. What are the counter-rhythms or narratives that are present in the organization and how can we hear and be curious about these views? What is behind the disruptive off-beat cow bell we hear every now and again from the manufacturing facility; is that worth exploring? Just getting interested in hearing these alternative rhythms is likely to leave us better equipped to adjust our own rhythm when it is needed.

Working in practice: Everyday creative disruption

Finding the disruption to our normal rhythms that helps train our edge can be a helpful team exercise too; and a great way of revealing what we normally do, and opening up possibilities for new ways of interacting. A good place to start is a regular team meeting. We work with a deck of cards with suggestions of small conversational acts which are intended to disrupt the normal rhythm of the meeting and patterns of conversation. Every five minutes each member of the team is given one card and they have five minutes to incorporate the suggestion into the flow of the meeting. The cards do not dictate "content" for the meeting, but rather small changes to how people participate in the conversation, for example, varying their pace, or volume; or changing posture; waiting longer to speak than they would normally; or not as long.

At the end of the meeting we design in 15 - 30 minutes to explore with the group what they noticed about the disruptions and their implications. What was helpful? What less helpful? What did the experience say about their normal rhythm? What might they like to keep from the experiment?

Concluding thoughts: Dancing not racing

We are struck by the paradoxical qualities of rhythm. It can be the binding or underpinning drive that you barely notice; the barely audible walking bass that holds the band together. At the same time it can be the whip-crack rimshot that draws our attention to endings, or beginnings, or just "news of difference". And as the *Grove* definition highlights, it has a fundamental quality to it. We talked earlier about human development in the womb and how our aural senses develop significantly before our visual sense. The first sounds we perceive are the rhythm of blood pumping through the ventricles of the mother's heart, and the inhalation and exhalation of breath. A steady-state, flowing rhythm lulls a baby to rest in the womb; and a punctuating rhythm, for example, a raised heart rate in the mother from a shock or surprise, may wake the baby – the rhythm that draws attention to disruption.

And our senses of rhythm heard and felt are very closely connected too. The footfall as the mother walks is audibly discerned, but also felt in the swaying movement of the biped by the baby in the womb. It is only more recently in human societies that we have brought in confusion by categorizing music and dance as separate things. They are fundamentally connected. And we think of Thelonious Monk whose tendency, when the music was really flowing, was to move away from the piano keyboard, in a sort of circling intuitive dance, conducting the band with his body (Kelley, 2010). He would suffer complaints that people had come to hear him play, not dance around. We suspect for Monk, this was a distinction that made little sense.

And if this sense of rhythm and movement is so fundamental to our (early) human experience, how might we, in our bands and organizations, become more attuned to the rhythms that continue to surround us. If we can learn to hear them more, then we can choose to go with them when they are helpful, and disrupt them when they are not. If we can recalibrate our sense of the paradoxical qualities of flow and punctuation in our leadership practices, this might give us many more options for variety, experimentation and change. And, perhaps more importantly, we might consider working with it as an underlying metaphor for how we live and work; life as a dance rather than a race could be a lot of fun.

8

Tone

You might like to read this while listening to:

Chitlins Con Carne, Kenny Burrell

Theme

Grove has multiple entries for tone, the initial listings focusing on the exact definition of a tone in terms of the musical intervals that make up the diatonic scale. However, the entry we are most interested in is also cross-referenced with the concept of "timbre":

Latin: tonus. A term describing the tonal quality of a sound; a clarinet and an oboe sounding the same note at the same loudness are said to produce different timbres. Timbre is a more complex attribute than pitch or loudness, which can be represented by a one-dimensional scale (high-low for pitch, loud-soft for loudness); the perception of timbre is a synthesis of several factors, and in computer-generated music considerable effort has been devoted to the creation and exploration of multi-dimensional timbral spaces.

(Timbre (tonus), *The Grove Dictionary of Music*, 2020)

With tone (or timbre) we are working with a more complex quality. It is something that happens beyond the notation of the sheet music. We can capture accurately the pitch and duration of the notes that we want played, and the volume with which we want them played. However, the sound that we experience when we listen to what comes out will not be entirely predictable. It will be affected by the material qualities of the instruments playing it. It will be affected by how the musicians interpret the dynamic instructions (the "volume control"). It may be affected by the acoustics of the performance space; and even by the prevailing atmospheric conditions during a performance as woods and metals respond to variances in temperature and humidity. And perhaps most of all it will be affected by the players. Grove draws attention to the tonal difference between the same note played at the same volume on an oboe and a clarinet. We would venture that the same note played at the same volume on the same clarinet by Sidney Bechet, and Jimmy Hamilton, would also demonstrate significant tonal differences.

We remember learning to play brass instruments. A version of the notes on the page came reasonably quickly, but it was years before something resembling a pleasant tone, let alone a unique tone, emerged. The particular musculature of the embouchure (the positioning of the lips in the mouthpiece) took time to set. The muscles used to produce and hold the embouchure took years to develop and strengthen, so that playing for more than short periods of time became possible. There is a deeply physiological and embodied side to the development of tone beyond the cerebral act of reading musical notation and translating it into the correct fingerings for the notes required. The tone you develop is a mixture of factors - the teachers you have had, the musical experiences, your own strength and physiology, even the dental accidents you have had or not had. And here we think of John Coltrane, who suffered with painful dental problems for years, but refused to see a dentist for fear that any interventions would change his tone on the saxophone. Tone is independent of and deeply influential on any piece of music you are playing.

And if we transfer this to an organizational context, perhaps we are starting to talk about qualities of leadership. If strategies and plans are our musical compositions, often we see organizations focus on developing leaders who can accurately reproduce the notes. Even when this is successful, and plans are executed to the letter, there is sometimes some frustration with the overall quality of the music. What can make a huge difference is shifting the emphasis beyond accurate reproduction of notes to developing leadership "tone". This is a leadership that draws on all of the experiences of learning to play, bringing in the voices of various teachers along the way, and embracing any idiosyncrasies of embouchure or style. It speaks to hard years learning a craft, and also hard yards finding a way to express individual qualities in an organizational context. And whilst we are emphasizing the individuality of tone here, this is not about playing solo, oblivious to all others. Musical arrangers, conductors, and instrumentalists talk about "blending tones"; finding ways to combine the unique qualities of individual voices to create something that truly transcends the notes on the page. Listening is at the heart of developing our own tone, and successfully bringing it in alongside others. Human organizations might be the equivalent of the "multi-dimensional timbral spaces" that computer-generated music has had to work so hard to try and simulate.

Variation: Appreciating tone

Developing tone on a musical instrument takes years of listening to yourself, reflecting on what you are hearing, and making small adjustments. It is often on the longer sustained notes that you can hear and develop tone more easily. In many ways it is a reflexive cybernetic process. And if we extend this to playing with others in an organizational context, then the same level of listening to others is important. However, it is all too easy to listen for the notes that we expect to hear in the musical score, and to miss interesting tonal qualities in the way others are playing. A similar danger is there for students of musicology, who may find themselves listening analytically to capture the harmonic structure of a piece, and noticing that they are missing the uniqueness and pleasure of the performance. Maybe the organizational equivalent here is remembering to surface from the Gantt chart or project plan once in a while, and also spend time being interested in *how* things are being carried out; are there any interesting or unexpected tonal qualities that might need appreciating, or developing?

There is often more going on than we notice with our eyes on the score. We are thinking now of the idea of overtones. Overtones are higher frequency components of any note being played at any given time. They may be part of the sound of the note being played, but normally we only hear the dominant tone. However, different musical traditions have ways of bringing these overtones to the fore. One of us was lucky enough to be introduced to the basics of Tuvan throat singing, or *khoomei*. The Tuvan people of southern Siberia have developed a technique of singing a fundamental bass note with a chest voice, and using the cavities of the throat and mouth to bring out the harmonically related overtones at higher pitches. The result is that they are able to produce multiple tones at once. In Tuvan throat song we are tuned into and hearing more of what is going on in the harmonic context than we would normally. Indeed for the Tuvans this form of music making has much to do with connection with the natural world. In their animistic tradition there is a spiritual appreciation of animals, plant life, landscape and their interrelationship which extends to their tonal as well as their physical properties. We also remember that another definition of overtone refers to connotation, suggestion, of a potentially political nature. In any context, there might be more going on if we can sharpen our senses. And whilst board rooms and factory floors may seem a far cry from the Siberian steppe, we might take inspiration from the Tuvans and try and listen for the overtones that are there.

Variation: Matching tone

In its definition of tone Grove draws attention to the tonal difference between instruments, in this case the oboe and the clarinet. Grove's definition of rhythm that we looked at in the previous chapter suggested changes in the rhythm or pitch of a piece of music fundamentally change the piece of music, whereas changes in the instrumentation don't. So, working at the level of tone, it seems we are not in the world of major transformation. However, we might be in the place of significantly changing the quality of the performance of what "is" (Beisser, 1970). Working with tone also seems to be about working in the present. It may also be about bringing to bear experiences from the past in the present, but fundamentally it is about listening and altering. We are back with the student brass musician playing long tones and listening for depth and difference. So, from an organizational perspective, this is perhaps about paying attention to how the organizational music is being played, rather than deciding to play something different. Tuning into what is going on in the moment is the key to opening up choices for alterations; not abandoning the piece altogether. And we think about a similar approach in the world of music therapy, the iso principle, a phrase first coined by psychiatrist and pioneer music therapist Ira Altshuler (Altshuler, 1948). Here, to aid changes in patients' mood states the therapist begins by identifying pieces of music which best match the current mood of the patient. They tune in carefully to the tonal world that the patient is experiencing, and try and come alongside this with music that blends with this tone. Rather than bluntly suggesting the patient change the piece of music ("if you're feeling down, whistle a happy tune...") it is a therapeutic technique that pays attention to what "is". Once this match in tone has been established, small shifts in the musical selection help to nudge the patient in the direction of a different mood state. There is a subtlety and nuance to this way of tonal working which we might also learn from in organization. Where we might hear the frustrated cry of "I don't understand why they can't just change their tune", going back to the iso principle and coming alongside the tone of what "is" rather than what "ought to be" might just help.

Working in practice: Congruence in tone

We worked with an organization whose purpose was to support and develop innova-tive science and technology start-ups, with a view to growing the sector for the benefit of 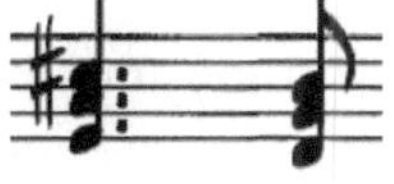 wider society. The ambition they had for the businesses they supported, and hopes for the growth of the market were compelling, and inspiring. However, internally, they had been noting a downward trend in staff engagement levels. Whilst their internal processes and working practices were well thought through and organized, upon inquiring widely across the organization it became clear that the "tone" of the work they were doing internally was very different to the "tone" of the ambition the organization expressed outwardly. How it felt to work there was very different to how it felt to be part of the innovation industry it was supporting. We began playing with the idea of the difference between the musical score, the notes you need to play as an organization, and playing with a tone that is congruent with what you espouse. The notes were all there. There were talent processes in place, performance management processes, processes to support staff growth and learning. However, when speaking to people about these they had become tick box exercises which had lost the lustre of their original intent. The notes were being played, but rather carelessly and lovelessly. What followed was a review of the internal processes which supported staff development, keeping the idea of the "tone of the performance" that was needed at the centre. We looked at ways of shaping talent conversations to capture some of the excitement, ambition and sense of possibility that the organization had for the innovation businesses that it supported. We looked at ways of shaping learning and development so as to capture some of the flavour of entrepreneurial "in the moment learning" that their clients embraced, rather than just offering a catalogue of courses. All this helped underpin and connect the day to day working in the organization, and their purpose in terms of supporting their clients. The "tone" between the "what" of their ambition and the "how" of their everyday working experience was much closer. This helped engagement, and encouraged a shift along the spectrum from just playing the notes to really performing.

Working in practice: Leadership as a tonal practice?

We've worked with a number of organizations over the years (a government body, a tax accountancy, a tech systems provider) who 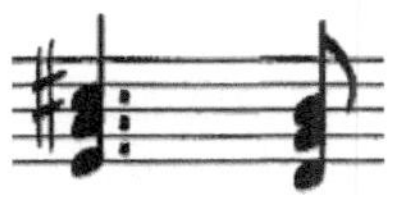 have been interested in reviewing their approach to learning and leadership development. With the best intentions in the world, over the years they had built up huge portfolios of development offerings in response to staff requests and needs. However, they had noticed that the breadth of their offerings, whilst impressive, was making them difficult to access and navigate; and also, that they were not seeing the shifts in leadership behaviours they had hoped for from all this effort and investment. In all cases, a lot of focus was placed on procuring high quality content in terms of the courses and programmes listed; yet somehow this had detracted from a focus on the experience of learning.

This puts us in mind of interviews and informal exchanges one of us had with jazz musicians Candy Dulfer, Han Bennink, and Willem Breuker. The conversations turned to the idea of jazz education and the relationship between expression and technique in the art form. How much technique is needed in order to play jazz? Which is more important, expression or technique? Is authentic expression on its own enough? Is there any point or possibility in jazz education? These are important conversations, and also run the risk of ending in binary positions with the idea of the technical craftsman at one end, and the muse-channelling mystic at the other. And we recognize the pattern of this discussion in the context of leadership development too. There is a narrative that says leaders are born not made, and that leadership is an expression of a natural talent. However, this framing de-emphasizes the value of being intentional in how we act into the complex systems of our organizations, and learning from the responses. Of course, we have a right to enact our selves, let our giant yawps out into the world, but done clumsily and without space for reflection, we may end up doing more harm than good. Theatre director Patsy Rodenburg talks about this mode of action as "third circle energy", where we risk pushing our personalities, foibles and all out in to the world with little thought for their impact (Rodenburg, 2008). This approach to leadership risks being expression without technique.

Operating from the other end of the spectrum, we could locate the management factories of MBA programmes at business schools around the world. Generations of managers are educated in the "propositional" technique of how to lead. The emphasis is often on models and frameworks, processes and procedures that provide the technical rule book of modern management. However, coming too much from this end of the spectrum we risk favouring technique over expression, and character, authenticity and tone of leadership are under-nourished.

Somehow, it seems to us, a combination of both is needed. Even Miles Davis, who created the conditions for some of the most admired spontaneous expressions captured on record, was often furious if players showed up not knowing his play book. Leading with real "tone" means finding ways of "being ourselves with skill". And supporting leaders in their learning and development means paying attention to both technique and expression.

With this shift in the framing of leadership in mind, we were able to work with these organizations to review their approach to leadership development. Sometimes this involved moving away from the idea of the leadership development team being responsible for cataloguing and administering as much content as possible, and moving towards the idea of curating a smaller offering which had a sense and meaning to it. Sometimes it meant adapting the way learning impact was measured, to embrace the qualitative and expressive sides of leadership, rather than just the mastery of content (or technique). And at other times, it meant rethinking the design of leadership development interventions altogether. It can be easy to think of leadership time as so valuable that any "programme" needs to be crammed with content to make the most of it. However, one organization was able to move towards the idea of designing for space to allow leaders the chance of having expressive experiences. Rather than focusing on the number of models mastered, it became enough for participants to have one or two "aha" moments, experiences that stood the chance of changing the qualities of their leadership, rather than simply giving them a new process or playbook to follow. Although these may all seem relatively minor shifts along the spectrum of technique versus expression, in all cases the changes caught the attention of learners, and gave them a more nuanced sense of what was expected of them as leaders from their respective organizations.

Working in practice: Tone in teams

Individuals can develop tone; but teams and whole organizations can have their dominant tones too. We worked alongside a senior leadership team at a biochemicals company. There had been some recent changes in the composition of the team as the organization had gained a few members in connection with a joint venture it had entered into as part of its growth strategy. The team were keen to spend some time reflecting on their working practices and dynamics as a group to ensure they were in good shape to lead the strategy. We held individual conversations with each of the team members, getting their sense of how the team operated. We also shadowed several team meetings to get a sense of the group dynamics for ourselves.

What we observed was a fairly high energy conversational culture. The team were mostly male, and there was a boisterousness that at its best was quite fun to be part of. However, we also noticed that in communication terms leaders seemed to be trading shots rather than really hearing what each other were saying, thinking up the next line and not building on ideas shared. The result seemed to be meetings that most enjoyed, but where little was moved on or developed in terms of the work agenda. This is not to say that work wasn't being done, it was just being done by the individual leaders in their own functional areas outside of meetings, not collectively. However, for the joint venture to be successful, finding ways of working effectively as a collective was vital.

What we also learned through the individual inquiry conversations was that the fast-paced verbal combat was "fun" on the one level, but it was also "the nip that denotes the bite" (Bateson, 1972, p. 180). The verbal jousting was both playful but also at times a way of sending a message of competing for dominance as each of the functional leaders held their own. There was a subtle undertone of threat to the playful interactions, which didn't lend itself to building the safe environment that is so helpful for creative collaboration. Showing uncertainty, experimenting with new approaches, or even revealing too much about their personal lives were all things individuals mentioned it being difficult to do.

With this in mind, one of the things we experimented with was a structure to alter the tone of their collective conversations. Whilst not outlawing the positive aspects of the fun and play, the aim was to give them an experience of different ways of being with one another, that might offer alternatives. We introduced them to the idea of story circles (Mead, 2014). All eight members of the team sat in a well-formed circle of chairs facing inwards so they could see each other. They each had three minutes (timed on an egg timer by the colleague to their right) to talk about an experience, personal or professional, where they had felt humbled through working together with someone. Three minutes was the time limit at which point the baton passed to the next person to speak. The rest of the group were to listen in silence. No questions were allowed. If the person stopped speaking before the three minutes had passed, the group sat in silence until the sands had run through. What followed was a structured 24 minutes of sharing and listening. The group were invited to speak from a more personal and vulnerable perspective, and the jockeying back and forth of their normal conversations was not allowed. As the stories were heard, the group seemed to take heart that they could share things with a more personal tone; not just from the perspective of "me the senior leader" but also the fuller human with a personal life, a past, a childhood, uncertainties and insecurities. After the circle had been completed, the group were invited to pair up and explore anything that they or others had shared that they were curious about, and these exploratory conversations went on for some time. Whilst the process was very controlled, it offered the team an experience of how they could interact with each other differently. They all took risks with what they shared to varying degrees. And with each risk taken it got a little bit safer to do so. In follow-up conversations a number of months later team members mentioned that the different sides of their colleagues that they had discovered in the story circle and subsequent discussions had helped them begin to build relationships on a different level. The nature of their team meetings hadn't completely changed, but a different tone had crept in, and more seemed possible beyond just verbal jousting.

Working in practice: Bringing out the overtones

Fourier analysis is a process that can be used to separate out the sound of a musical instrument into its constituent sine or cosine waves. It can take, for example, the sound of 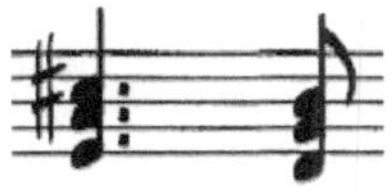 the oboe from our Grove definition, and isolate the dominant and supplementary parts of the sound wave that the oboe produces. However, if we isolate and amplify the dominant part of the sound wave, we don't get a sound that we recognize as the oboe at all. The quality which we perceive as "oboe" lies as much in the minor and supplementary parts of the sound wave as it does in the dominant aspects.

Amongst others the company Korg realized this when developing synthesizers in the 70s and 80s. To get something close to an authentic tone, they were having to add more and more "messiness" back in, even to the extent of having a function for overlaying the sound of a human intake of breath prior to the notes being voiced. As sophisticated as the technology was, even they realized that getting an authentic sound, short of sampling live oboe playing, was going to be extremely tough.

So, if these messy overtones are what we recognize at some fundamental level as part of a true and authentic sound, in organizational terms this might speak to us all trying to be less perfect. Text book organizational practices and processes might allow us to reproduce the dominant elements of the sound wave reasonably competently, but without the nuances of the supplementary tones the sound is off. Perhaps these supplementary aspects come from our personal history, family story, hobbies and interests, sense of humor, anxieties, character quirks. Social constraints and expectations in human organizations can be effective Fourier analysis processes in their own right, identifying aspects of ourselves which aren't part of the dominant organizational tone and inviting us to leave our supplementary tones at home. The result might be compliant or even consistent, but risks sounding flat.

What can help here, is reflective work to understand and bring to the fore aspects of our personalities and identities that we might have knowingly or unknowingly hidden. It might be the inner birdwatcher Bateson was keen to see evidence of before lending a politician enough trust to vote for them. And if we think about the teams we work in, considering the tone of the different members that make up the team might help us to put together more diverse and creative groups. Band leader Duke Ellington was famous for recruiting and composing for the individual sounds of his musicians. He did not compose lines for trumpet – he composed lines for Cootie Williams, or Cat Anderson, or Clark Terry. He knew how to write not for the dominant tone that is "trumpet", but for the subtleties and nuances of these individuals on that instrument. In an organizational context, we might substitute the role of "trumpet" for that of engineering lead, or procurement specialist. How might we compose a team based on the unique tonal qualities of the individuals in these roles, not just the empty clothes of their job descriptions?

Developing tone is necessarily a reflective practice, which is not always an easy mode to get into amidst the pace of much organizational life. We often find it helpful to give people a light structure to get started. We ask individuals to take stock of people and situations that have influenced and shaped them. For example, they might spend some time combing through their experiences from childhood, through school, into the workplace. We ask them to list the people who have influenced them chronologically (and this may include influential thinkers and writers, not just people we know personally). Then for each person we ask them to list the qualities that stand out for them when they think of them. What do they admire about this individual? What about them would they like to emulate? We ask them to think about how they might bring some of each person's qualities to bear in their own life. And then for a specific challenge they are facing, we ask them to think about how one or more of their list might approach it.

This process focuses outwards on the teachers and influencers in our lives. However, the connections made through addressing the questions naturally invite reflections on how these "teachers" have shaped who we are today, even if we silence some of these qualities in an organizational context. Our personalities are shaped in different ways by all the interactions we have; so it stands to reason that these people that really stand out for us will have released an echo that might still be discernible amongst the supplementary parts of our soundwaves. Getting back in touch with these can allow us to choose which of these we want to amplify and more consciously bring into our day to day practice. And when facing complex and challenging organizational contexts it can be reassuring to know that we have our teachers at our backs.

Working in practice: Facilitating an upstream conversation on tone

When teams work together to develop strategies and strategic implementation plans, a lot of detailed work is often done around timelines and what needs to be car-  ried out when and by whom. This is admirable and helpful, however, may only amount to agreeing the notes to be played, and in which order. The work stops at laying out a score for the music to be played, but often gives little thought to how they would like the performance to be. The focus is on the "what" and less on the "how". In some instances, teams do become interested in the "how" of their strategic delivery, and they may choose to think about this quality using the metaphor of culture. Helpful as the culture metaphor can be, we have also found it useful to work with the concept of "tone" as the generative image for thinking about how a group want to perform together.

One way we have approached this is by asking individuals in a team to choose from selections of short soundbites of different types of music. Some might be loud, or soft; major, minor or dissonant; have different instrumentation, different tempi; feature legato or staccato playing. We ask them to choose a soundbite which speaks to some aspect of how they currently perform together as a team, then a second soundbite which speaks to how they need to perform together to do justice to the "score" of their strategy. We then get curious as a group and inquire into what drew people to choose various soundbites. What emerges in discussion is a rich sense of the sort of tone the team currently perform with, and a statement of aspiration and intent for the tonal qualities they feel they need in their work together.

Extending the metaphor further we might talk about sound engineering and signal to noise ratio. In this context, if the signal is the tonal sound you want to come through on a recording, there is a certain proportion of "noise" (sounds other than those you intended) that can be tolerated before your intended sound is compromised. In an organizational context it is unlikely that everyone's behaviours will shift overnight to be in tune with any expected strategic performance. However, if enough people are performing the signal, and focus on amplifying the qualities that are needed, then the sound you are after may still be achievable, even if there is other organizational noise going on. This can be a reassuring thought to hang onto, particularly in large organizations where change can easily seem overwhelming.

Hand in hand with good planning, this type of "upstream" conversation early on can be something that teams can go back to in order to make sure the tones they produce from the notes on the page result in the type of performance they can be proud of.

Concluding thoughts: The mastering process

We are conscious that much of our work and musings on the idea of tone has its roots in reflective practice at an individual level. The Grove definition locates tone at the level of the individual instrument. And there is much richness and fascination in working with individuals to help them realize and reveal the uniqueness of their own tonal voices.

However, we are also reflecting on pitfalls from the mastering process in the recording studio. Earlier recordings, for example the recording of *Kind of Blue*, relied much on the skill and art of the studio technicians in placing microphones at the right distances to try and get some balance of sound on the tapes. They worked with the constraints of the room, in the case of the *Kind of Blue* recordings the acoustics of the Armenian orthodox church which Columbia was using as a studio. As digital recording techniques developed, technicians were able to focus much more accurately on isolating the sounds of individual instruments, and working to enhance them later in the mastering suite. As the number of tracks it was possible to record increased, rather than having an individual track for the drum kit, you might find each sound of the kit split out and recorded as separate digital channels. In post-production the sound of the snare could be manipulated separately from the sound of the crash cymbal, the bass drum rounded out, and the ride given more reverb. The possibilities were endless. However, when we were working in recording studios, on a number of occasions we noticed that, when the individual tracks were put back together, the overall result was lack-lustre. In the world of possibility available at the level of enhancing the sound of the individual instruments, technicians were in danger of losing touch with a sense of the overall tonal qualities of the performance. The recordings that benefited most from the technological advances were led by teams who always kept one ear out for the sound that the whole band was making together, as well as working at the detailed level.

And this is true of working in organizations too. It can be worthwhile and rewarding to work with individuals and teams; enhancing their tonal contributions at a local level. However, the whole organizational performance needs to be worth listening to. If we don't keep our ear to the overall sound, then the risk of unintended dissonances creeping in is always there. And it is to this overall sound that we pay more attention next.

9

Back in the mix

Jazz exemplifies artistic activity that is at once individual and communal, performance that is both repetitive and innovative, each participant sometimes providing background support and sometimes flying free.

Mary Catherine Bateson

You might like to read this while listening to:

Moanin', Art Blakey & The Jazz Messengers

Argentinian writer Jorge Luis Borges once shared with amusement an entry he'd found in a Chinese encyclopaedia with French philosopher Michel Foucault. The entry listed categories into which animals can be sorted, including "(a) belonging to the Emperor, (b) embalmed, (c) tame, (d) sucking pigs, (e) sirens, (f) fabulous, (g) stray dogs, (h) included in the present classification, (i) frenzied, (j) innumerable, (k) drawn with a very fine camel hair brush (l) *etc*, (m) having just broken the water pitcher, (n) that from a long way off look like flies." (Barron, Montuori, Barron et al, 1997, p. 108). For Borges this was a source of exotic amusement. What Foucault saw was a taxonomy that showed the limitations of "European" ways of thinking about animals. Our taxonomy has been limited here too. In the last four chapters we've broken down the concept of music and sound into melody, harmony, rhythm and tone in order to play with them, rather than because these categories represent any sort of reliable truth. At best, it is an incomplete truth, as we're sure we could have just as interestingly explored aspects of music and sound such as:

- Resonance
- Dynamics
- Dissonance
- Consonance
- Theme and variation
- Noise

We'd encourage you to play with these and others in your thought experiments, and in your practice.

And of course, in taking the idea of sound and music apart, we miss the fact that we need to consider it as a whole. The world is a messy ensemble improvisation and there is much going on at the same time. And to pick up a thread from earlier, one ensemble improvisation we turn to again and again for insight is the Miles Davis album *Kind of Blue*.

As we know, the album was recorded in two short studio sessions in a deconsecrated Armenian church in New York City in March and April 1959. The musicians were assembled at short notice, most squeezing the recording sessions in between other gigs. The five tracks of the album were almost all recorded in one take, and represent some of the finest improvised music ever captured. Viewing the musical ensemble for these recordings as a temporary organization, what might we learn?

Taking a step back from the situation, success seems far from guaranteed. None of the musicians knew what they would be recording, even after Miles had handed out scraps of paper with the modal scales they were to use to improvise from. However, what stands out for us, as the difference that makes the difference, is their stance or orientation to the work they came together to do. They showed up with the willingness to pay attention together to what happens once they start to play, and to develop it as best they can. And this orientation seems to us to be the commonality which gives them a platform from which to work together, in spite of the many differences we could highlight (e.g. different instruments, fingerings, techniques, traditions, experience and status in the industry, levels of relationship with each other, energy). We might call it the improvisational stance; and in using the word stance we're also imagining something of the boxer or the dancer. We're imagining contact with the give of the boxing canvas, or the sprung boards of the stage. Feet planted, but not too firmly; balanced, but ready to respond and move in any direction lightly as needed.

Hearing the whole system

Another way in which we sometimes think about improvising ensembles is as dynamic systems. We mentioned earlier the Macy Conferences, a series of events run in the 40s and 50s in New York which deliberately brought together thinkers from "unconnected" fields. Hopefully not putting it too crudely, their intention was to try and put everything "back in the mix", to arrive at new (or old) understandings through the connections and relationships between things, rather than their taxonomic distinctions. This field of connective inquiry was often referred to as cybernetics, which Norbert Wiener defines as "the scientific study of control and communication in the animal and the machine" (Wiener, 1948, p. 19). They drew widely on different disciplines to try and understand how complex systems regulated, constrained and enabled themselves. Where systems are unable to regulate themselves, they dissipate or entropy. Where the system over-regulates itself, the result is stagnation or stasis. What is required to maintain a healthy or viable system is what cyberneticist Ashby referred to as "requisite variety" (Ashby, 1956, pp. 202-218). It is a level of "difference" with which the system can work without becoming overwhelmed and descending into chaos. In the context of *Kind of Blue*, had Miles Davis simply said to the band members to start playing, there would very likely have been too much variety, and the result would have been cacophony. Had he stipulated that they all play in unison on a C major chord only, the result would have been dull and unvaried. In offering the light structure of the modal scales, and indicating the order of the solos as the pieces unfolded, he created a container that allowed for enough variety to be held. The result is a temporal audible construction which we recognize as the sextet performing together and improvising something worth listening to. They are dancing on the edge. And at times may be a cybernetic hair's breadth away from cacophony or stagnation, but this is part of the thrill.

And if we translate this to our organizational experiences, perhaps we can recognize times when the system has been overregulated, and things have felt slow, or stale, or stagnant; times when it has been hard to innovate or experiment. And also times when things have been too loose and confusion has been the result; people everywhere playing in different keys and different rhythms. And hopefully we can also recognize those times when things have come together and we have been able to be open to enough variety, to manage the dynamic stability of a truly viable system. These are usually team experiences that can nourish those who were part of them for many years to come.

Leading ensemble improvisation

And as we think of the thrill of the successful (or probably better, succeeding...) ensemble improvisation we note that thrill is closely related to risk and courage. Viable systems are always at the edge trying to maintain a course between the Scylla and Charybdis of stagnation and dissolution. Leading and participating in these contexts requires a certain liminal position or stance. Patricia Shaw talks about leadership being "the courage to take action when you don't know how it will ripple out" (Shaw, 2017). There is a stepping into the unknown that needs to happen. Improviser Keith Johnstone talks about there being two types of people, those who say no and are "rewarded by the certainty they achieve" and those who say yes, and are "rewarded by the adventures that they have" (Johnstone, 1981, p. 92). This is a wry simplification for effect, but does speak to the all too human tendency at times to avoid variety and choose stagnation over taking a risk.

Jazz musician and management professor, Frank Barrett, writes in *Yes to the Mess* (Barrett, 2012) of an "aha" experience of risk-taking in his early days teaching at Harvard Business School. Having carefully prepared lesson plans and learning outcomes for his sessions at the prestigious school, one day a student asked a question that had little to do with the plan. Rather than brush over it he took the risk of following the curiosity of the question. In doing so, in hindsight he realized they had covered the topic far more deeply and richly than he could ever have hoped for had he stuck to the lesson plan. This was an experience of working on the edge between cybernetic stagnation and entropy which really shaped his thinking about leading and learning in organizations as ensemble improvisations.

And given that stagnation and entropy are always possibilities, there is something about the role of calibrating our leadership experiences which helps keep us in the space of viable and creative systemic work. Barrett describes leadership being about relational moves in an unfolding context, where actions create feedback which informs the next step. This is very much a calibration that needs to take place from within the situation (prior analysis is not a relevant option). It requires an openness and a vulnerability (an openness to the potential of "wounding") to step into the mix and try and work out what is the right thing to do next. And it is a muscle we can develop if we seek out the right stretch experiences. To give you an example of what we mean, here is a small story from one of us...

Bringing this to life – The BIMHUIS story

It was the early 90's in Amsterdam. Clutching a newly bought tenor saxophone (a Selmer Bundy II), and hardly able to play it, I found myself walking through the doors of the old BIMHUIS jazz club. They were running a thing called an open jazz workshop, and a mix of curiosity and fear had brought me there. I sat anxiously at the bar outside, hearing sounds coming from the performance area, waiting my turn. Inside, I was greeted by the sight of about 50 people on stage. There was a rhythm section, some trumpets and other brass, and about 30 saxophone players, beginners through to more advanced. The group struck up a blues number, and someone encouraged me to take my saxophone out of the case and join them on stage. I stepped into the group and spent time finding my space, listening to them playing and sensing into the vibe. The band leader was taking them through chorus after chorus, as more and more players got their fingers round the main tune and started making music together. I too was beginning to find my way, settling in, even starting to enjoy it a bit. And then I noticed the band leader signalling for a line to be formed at the front of the stage. I felt a lurch in the pit of my stomach. One by one players were invited to step forward to the microphone to take a solo chorus. The dynamics of crowd movement on the stage saw me being nudged towards the line, and my anxiety locked into a sort of reverb hum. My turn came, and I managed to try a simple repeated bluesy phrase; turning it over and over across the rhythm and noticing it change with its context. And I felt the support at my back as others listened, and shouted encouragement. The reverb hum tilted into a building excitement. The anxiety of leaping into the void was shifting into the sheer joy of developing my voicein the midst of the energy and the emerging tune.

And then it was over. The band leader gruffly reminded us each to leave two guilders on the bar counter on the way out, one for the light, one for the heat. And out we filed into the cold late autumn evening; still making sense of the intensity of the experience of being held by the group, and feeling learning happen live with all the joy and anxiety that went with it. And, in our own quiet ways, each resolving to practice more, and return to find this experience again.

We need *enough* variety to develop what Barrett refers to as "provocative competence" (Barrett, 2012, p. 139). Finding this sweet-spot can be tricky, and in the example above, the role of the band leader as convenor and holder of the space is significant in creating the conditions for stretch learning. We are wary of models, but sometimes when we are scanning the organizational contexts we are working in, we imagine the most helpful improvisational stance and actions as being a combination of the following qualities:

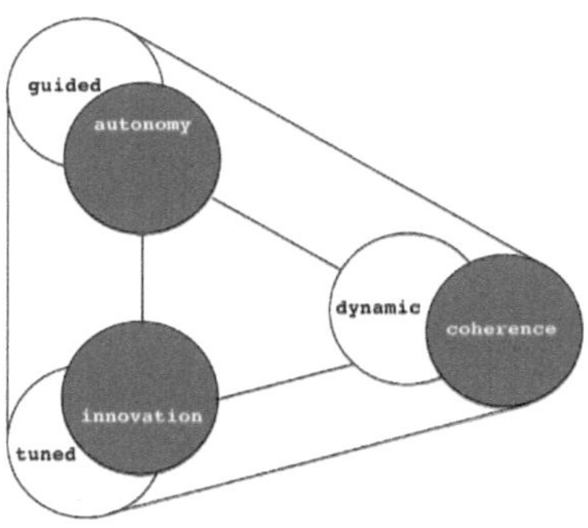

In his work on reinventing organizations, Frederic Laloux talks about autonomy, coherence and evolutionary purpose being vital to allow a modern organization to thrive and adapt in a complex environment (Laloux 2014). We agree with much of this; and are a little afraid of the tendency of nouns to try and solidify things. If we are to maintain the moving stillness of the improvisational stance, then we needed to free them up again with some complexifying adjectives.

Our build on Laloux incorporates:

Guided autonomy: enough freedom to act, but with enough of a guide or agreed constraint to ensure that the collective action is not chaotic.

Tuned innovation: developing novelty and newness in terms of actions not at random, or for their own sake, but connected with news of difference in relationship with your organizational context.

Dynamic coherence: striving towards a wholeness of collective action that doesn't cease to evolve and change at the point that it considers itself to be whole; a leading and following that coheres as it shifts; almost the organizational equivalent of a murmuration of starlings.

There is tension inherent in all of these pairings; and it is keeping the tension alive in our collective actions which helps maintain the life that is in any viable system. Any of the words without the modifying relationship to its pairing would send us towards either stagnation or entropy. Leading "back in the mix" seems to us to be about developing our skill at holding some of these tensions in a place which is generative. It is the instinct that informed Miles Davis's choices when bringing the band into the studio for the *Kind of Blue* sessions, leading to recordings which changed how we think about music. It is the instinct that brought the Macy Conferences into being, with the tension of transdisciplinary thinking advancing knowledge and progress in numerous areas. And whilst we have been working extensively with the idea of sound and music, we can't help feeling that Mondrian's *Broadway Boogie Woogie* (1942 – 1943) captures it better than we can, with the energy of life and music contained and sustained in the wider system of the city:

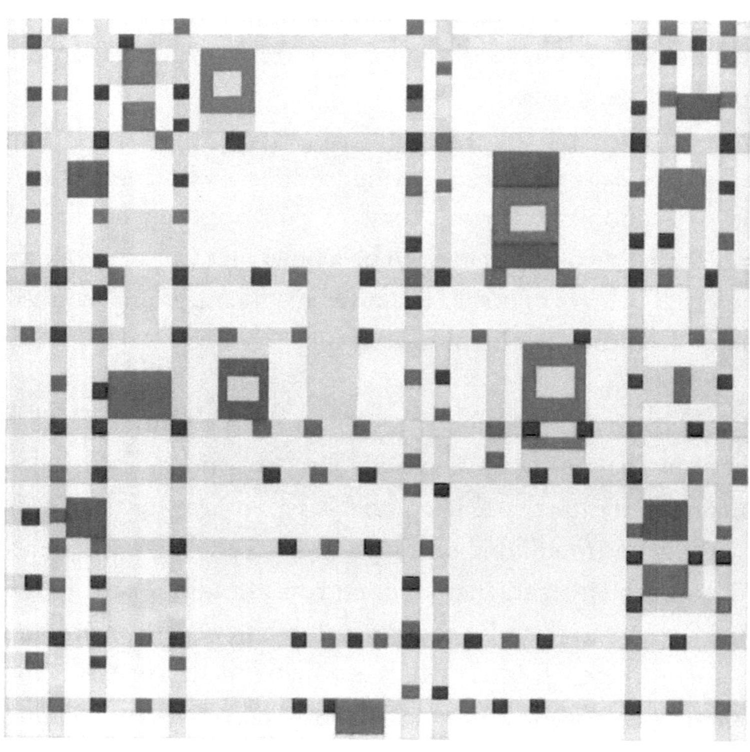

Piet Mondrian, Broadway Boogie Woogie (1942 - 1943),
MOMA

10

From re-wiring to re-sounding and beyond

Those who shun the whimsy of things will experience rigor mortis before death

Tom Robbins

You might like to read this while listening to:

Cool Struttin', Sonny Clark

We began by exploring the idea that many of the challenges we face in organizations and societies more widely can be thought of as problems of perspective. We seem to be living in an age of the politics of assertion. Power seems to rest with those who can uphold a dominant perspective as the only truth available. And operating from one perspective only is a fairly limited way of being in the world. The more tightly we cling to one frame or version of events, the harder it becomes for us to entertain different perspectives. And one of the results of this is the increasing polarization in viewpoints we hear around a number of important topics, be that climate, economics, or how we should work with the displaced peoples of the world. Social constructionist thinking, whilst not new to this century, is more relevant than ever, if we are to learn the lesson more widely that we are deeply implicated in the challenges that we face as participants. Arguing for the relevance and validity of perspectives other than the dominant narratives of those with power, is important work; and applies as much to power with a small "p" in our everyday interactions as it does to the large-scale political stage.

From here we noted that dominant perspectives on organizational life abound too. Organizations (and work in organizations) are broadly viewed as rational, plannable, and with enough effort, predictable. Where things don't go as planned, this is a technical glitch, which, with enough expertise, can be analysed and remedied. This perspective operates from a metaphor of engineering or electronics. And in this context any change or development work equates to a re-wiring of the whole.

And whilst this way of thinking about organization has a lot to offer (for example its emphasis on the value of pre-thought, and clarity), we noted that it didn't speak fully to our own experiences of the messiness of organizational life. In light of the complexity of our experiences of working in organizations, Stacey's (and others') views of organizations as complex responsive processes also seemed to get closer to what we have been living. From this perspective, organizational patterns are reinforced or altered by the gestures and responses we make; and our conversational gestures and responses are particularly significant and deserve our attention. If this is the stuff that we are using to weave "organization" then **in times of change maybe "re-sounding" not "re-wiring" is an alternative way of thinking about what it is we need to do together.** Paying attention to what we are doing now is the place to start. What are we saying to each other and not saying, hearing and not hearing? And using the key ingredients of that most heightened form of sound, music, might provide a more nuanced metaphor that does some justice to the sophisticated and complex relational and emotional qualities of organization.

An opening not a closing

As we approach the end of this short book, "good practice" and well-intentioned advice ring in our ears suggesting that a satisfying overview and closing is probably in order. However, we notice that this awakens in us anxieties about having to be summative, definitive, and conclusive. Our experience of writing this is deeply connected with how we first started to work together. It began with play, and an instinct that putting things together in unusual combinations is usually an interesting thing to do. At first it was unconventional ways of playing musical instruments. Then it became regular conversations which ranged widely via associations and adjacent connections. We used to apologize for these "digressions" until we managed to persuade our inner critical voices that perhaps departing from the way was an interesting and valuable thing to do. And those inner critical voices have not entirely disappeared as we have riffed on and explored these themes further throughout the writing process. "Couldn't you do something, more normal, more logical?", they say; but for the most part hopefully we have managed not to listen.

What we have tried to do here in writing is share some of the qualities of these associative conversations that we have been having and continue to have. We offer the idea of the sound metaphor as something that we hope others of you will feel like exploring and playing with. We set our own creative constraint in taking Melody, Harmony, Rhythm and Tone as sub-metaphors for thinking about alternative ways of organization. What has made it to the page is informed by our own experiences and consulting practices. And we are aware that on a different day, given the same frame, different associations and connections may have stood out for us. At most we'd consider this a head arrangement (minimal musical structure used by jazz combos), and certainly not a full musical score; an utterance, not a summation.

And perhaps the most significant thing that we have learned and are still learning is further "upstream" than this, and has to do with what we have come to call the Batesonian instinct. At our best, we hope we've been able to get in touch with a fundamental instinct to combine things that "don't belong together", and explore them with genuine curiosity. It is a child-like instinct which is quickly bred out of us, and leaves us susceptible to those who would convince us of their singular truths. But more than that, our hunch is that it is following this instinct that will help us, in our organizations and societies, find creative solutions to some of the challenges we face.

Where to next?

We are reminded that the root of the word cybernetics is related to the Greek *kybernetes*, or steersman. When steering a course across a body of water, the desired end point may be known, but getting there involves thousands of in-the-moment micro adjustments to the rudder. Currents, tide, and weather conditions are in constant flux and the adjustments that are needed cannot be fully calculated in advance. We are perhaps nearing some kind of shore now, however, we notice our thoughts turning to where next. Increasingly in our explorations of sound and music we have found ourselves in the world of the embodied, through dance or choreography, or even sound production in the area of the throat! The inner critical voices said that this was unconnected because we set out to explore sound. And, again, we notice that this is the imperative to fragment making itself felt. Over time (western) music has become separated from dance, movement and the embodied. Originally, the production of musical sound and rhythm began with the bodies of the participants, through their voices, hand clapping, foot stomping etc. Sound and music were produced by the collective for the collective. It is only later that "musician" becomes a specialist role, and the idea of the musician being separate from the audience evolves.

Special spots are cleared for them in village halls, stages are erected for them to stand on. And gradually music moves towards being a specialist commodity consumed by an audience which does not participate in its production, no longer the collective endeavour of a swaying crowd. This seems to us to be another journey of disintegration. We have placed ourselves outside of the music making, in the same way that we are often tempted to place ourselves outside of any responsibility for an organization or society's problems and challenges. What might happen if we find ways to reintegrate these things that have been separated? If we can explore organization through sound and music, what happens if we take seriously the embodied experience of organization as dance? What might a deep and intuitive somatic approach to Organization Development look like? What else have we disallowed ourselves that might be helpful to reintegrate into our practices? There will be people out there who already know far more about this than us. And we are aware that they may not all sit in the organizational science departments of established universities. Wherever they are we look forward to finding them and exploring more.

Oxford, Görlitz & Amsterdam, September, 2020

	1	2	3	4	5
Melody	Melody in teams	Hearing the counter-tune	The human note	Training the listening muscle	Melodic metaphor
Harmony	Setting the harmonic tone	Creating space for harmonic relationships between notes	Listening for harmonic nuance	Training the ear	Creating harmonic space
Rhythm	Designing for breaks in the rhythm	Finding the perfect rhythm?	Rhythm and comping	Learning to hear polyrhythms	Everyday creative disruption
Tone	Congruence in tone	Leadership as a tonal practice?	Tone in teams	Bringing out the overtones	Facilitating an upstream conversation on tone

Altshuler. I. (1948). A psychiatrist's experiences with music as a therapeutic agent. In D.M. Schullian & M. Schoen (Eds), *Music and medicine* (pp. 266-281). Henry Schuman.

Ashby, W. R. (1952). *Design for a brain*. Chapman & Hall.

Ashby, W. R. (1956). *An introduction to cybernetics*. Chapman & Hall.

Baines, A. C. (2021). Drone. In *Grove Music Online*. Oxford University Press. https://www.oxfordmusiconline.com/grovemusic/view/ 10.1093/gmo/9781561592630.001.0001/ omo-9781561592630-e-0000008192

Barrett, F. (2012). *Yes to the mess: Surprising leadership lessons from jazz.* Harvard Business Review Press.

Barron, F., Montuori, A., & Barron, A. (1997). *Creators on creating: Awaking and cultivating the imaginative mind*. Penguin.

Bateson, G. (1972). *Steps to an ecology of mind*. The University of Chicago Press.

Bateson, G. (2002). *Mind and nature: A necessary unity.* Hampton Press.

REFERENCES

Bateson, G., & Bateson, M. C. (2004). *Angels fear: Towards an epistemology of the sacred*. Hampton Press.

Beisser, A. (1970). *The paradoxical theory of change*. http://www.gestalt.org/arnie.htm

Blake, W. (1994). *The works of William Blake: Auguries of innocence*. Wordsworth Editions.

Campbell, M. (2021). Timbre. In *Grove Music Online*. Oxford University Press. https://www.oxfordmusiconline.com/grovemusic/view/10.1093/gmo/9781561592630.001.0001/omo-9781561592630-e-0000027973?rskey=XYnB2T&result=1

Capra, B. (Director). (1990). *Mindwalk* [Film]. Triton Pictures.

Charlton, N. (2008). *Understanding Gregory Bateson: Mind, beauty and the sacred earth*. State University of New York Press.

Ciborra, C. (1999). Notes on improvisation and time in organizations. *Accounting, Management and Information Technologies, 9* (2), 77-94

Cohn, R., Hyer, B., Dahlhaus, C., Anderson, J., & Wilson, C. (2021). Harmony. In *Grove Music Online*. Oxford University Press. https://www.oxfordmusiconline.com/grovemusic/view/10.1093/gmo/9781561592630.001.0001/omo-9781561592630-e-0000050818

Cooperrider, D., Whitney, D., & Stavros, J. (2008). *Appreciative Inquiry Handbook* (2nd ed.). Crown Customs.

Csikszentmihalyi, M. (1990). *Flow: The Psychology of Optimal Experience*. Harper and Row.

Dorst, K. (2015). *Frame innovation: Create new thinking by design*. The MIT Press.

Geertz, C. (1973). *The interpretation of cultures: Selected essays.* Basic Books.

Gergen, K. J. (2009). *An invitation to social construction* (2nd ed.). Sage.

Goethe, J. W. (1840). *Goethe's Theory of Colours; translated from the German: with notes by Charles Lock Eastlake, R.A., F.R.S.* John Murray. (Original work published 1810).

Heifetz, R., Linsky, M., & Grashow, A. (2009). *Leadership in a permanent crisis.* Harvard Business Review.

Herman, S. M., & Korenich, M. (1977). *Authentic management: A Gestalt orientation to organizations and their development.* Addison-Wesley.

Heron, J., & Reason, P. (2008). Extending epistemology within a co-operative inquiry. In P. Reason & H. Bradbury (Eds.), *The SAGE handbook of action research: Participative inquiry and practice* (2nd ed., pp. 366-380). Sage.

HOK (2020). Retrieved from https://www.hok.com/projects/view/the-francis-crick-institute/

iRockJazz (2013). *The great jazz debate: What is jazz?* https://www.youtube.com/watch?v=H1lrUF6Az70&feature=share&list=PL536C79699F14C0A0

Johnstone, K. (1981). *Impro: Improvisation and the theatre.* Methuen Drama.

Johnstone, K. (1999). *Impro for storytellers.* Faber & Faber.

Kantor, D. (2012). *Reading the room: Group dynamics for coaches and leaders.* Jossey-Bass.

REFERENCES

Kelley, R. D. G. (2010). *Thelonius Monk: The life and times of an American original*. Free Press.

Korzybski, A. (1994). *Science and sanity: An introduction to non-Aristotelian systems and general semantics* (5th ed.). Institute of General Semantics.

Lakoff, G., & Johnson, M. (2003). *Metaphors we live by*. University of Chicago Press.

Laloux, F. (2014). *Reinventing organizations: A guide to creating organizations inspired by the next stage of human consciousness*. Nelson Parker.

London, J. (2021). Rhythm. In *Grove Music Online*. Oxford University Press. https://www.oxfordmusiconline.com/grovemusic/view/10.1093/gmo/9781561592630.001.0001/omo-9781561592630-e-0000045963

McNiff, J. (2002). *Action research for professional development: Concise advice for new action researchers*. http://www.jeanmcniff.com/ar-booklet.asp

Mead, G. (2014). *Telling the story: The heart and soul of successful leadership*. John Wiley & Sons.

Metalogue. (2018). *Organization transformation: "Fateful framings"*. https://metalogue.co.uk/Metalogue-Report-on-Transformation-Dec-2018.pdf

Mingus, C. (1998). *Beneath the underdog*. Canongate.

Montuori, A. (2005). Gregory Bateson and the promise of transdisciplinarity. *Cybernetics and Human Knowing, 12*(1-2), 147-158.

Morgan, G. (1997). *Images of organization*. Sage.

Nachmanovitch, S. (1981). *Gregory Bateson: Old men ought to be explorers.* http://www.batesonsymposium.com/Writings/Nachmanovitch.Bateson.Old.Men.Ought.To.Be.Explorers.d.pdf

Nachmanovitch, S. (1990). *Free play: Improvisation in life and art.* Penguin.

Pearce, W. B. (1989). *Communication and the human condition.* Southern Illinois University Press.

Pelligrini, C. A. (2017). *Time-outs and their role in improving safety and quality in surgery.* Bulletin of the American College of Surgeons.https://bulletin.facs.org/2017/06/time-outs-and-their-role-in-improving-safety-and-quality-in-surgery/

Reich, S. (1972) *Clapping Music* – performance (Steve Reich and Kristjan Järvi, Paris, 2014). https://www.youtube.com/watch?v=1EQjO2yrWyc

Ringer, A. (2021). Melody. In *Grove Music Online.* Oxford University Press. https://www.oxfordmusiconline.com/grovemusic/view/10.1093/gmo/9781561592630.001.0001/omo-9781561592630-e-0000018357

Robbins, T. (1980). *Still life with woodpecker.* Bantam Books.

Rodenburg, P. (2008). *The second circle: How to use positive energy for success in every situation.* Norton

Roth, G. (2004). *Connections: The five threads of intuitive wisdom.* Tarcher. https://www.5rhythms.com/gabrielle-roths-5rhythms/

Rowe, D. E., & Schulmann, R. (2007). *Einstein on politics.* Princeton University Press.

REFERENCES

Scharmer, C. O. (2018). *The essentials of theory U: Core Principles and Applications.* Berrett-Koehler.

Shakespeare, W. (1962). *The players' Shakespeare: Macbeth.* Heinemann.

Shaw, M. (2018). *The wandering court.* Westcountry School of Myth. https://schoolofmyth.com/five-weekend-programme/

Shaw, P. (2002). *Changing conversations in organizations: A complexity approach to change.* Routledge.

Shaw, P. (2017). *Be the change.* https://www.youtube.com/watch?v=la2h9yCd6Qs&t=1s

Snowden, D., & Boone, M. (2007). A leader's framework for decision making. *Harvard Business Review, 85*(11), 68-76.

Stacey, R. (2003). Organizations as complex responsive processes of relating. *Journal of Innovative Management, 8*(2), 27-39.

Terry, C. (2007). *Clark: The autobiography of Clark Terry.* University of California Press.

Watts, A. (2018). An introduction to metaphysics [Lecture]. (particularly from 12 minutes 46 seconds) https://www.youtube.com/watch?v=iC3SNXHwTcU

Whitney, D. (2010). Appreciative Inquiry: Creating spiritual resonance in the workplace. *Journal of Management, Spirituality & Religion 7*(1), 73-88.

Wiener, N. (1948). *Cybernetics: Or control and communications in the animal and the machine.* MIT Press.

Williams, R. (2009). *The blue moment.* Faber & Faber.

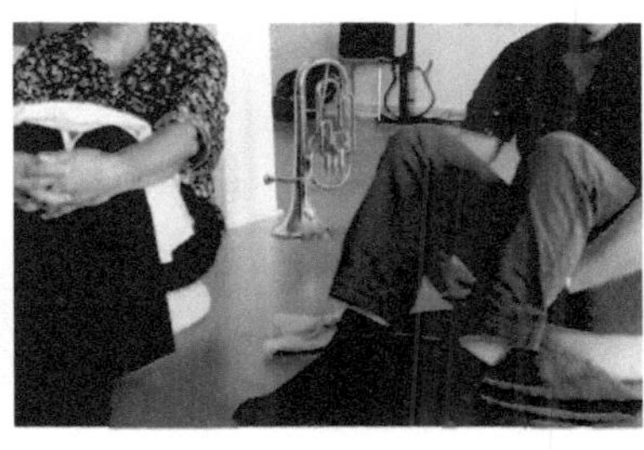

Rik Spann is an organizational consultant, applied musicologist, artist and jazz musician. In his work he is interested in exploring what happens at the crossroads of various fields, including science, art, design, music, theatre, dance, film and beyond. He also loves to play with weird combinations, humor, paradox, everyday life, blue notes, and stuff that can't be defined. He lives in Amsterdam, The Netherlands, with a view of a canal, his sons and girlfriend in his heart, and a guitar in his hands.

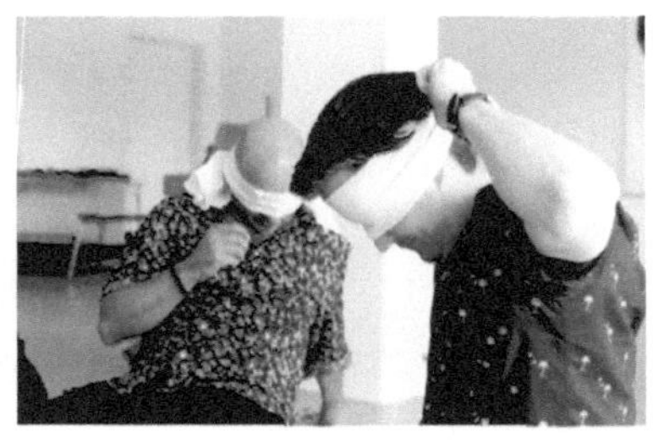

Simon Martin is an organizational consultant, keen flugelhornist, and Partner at Metalogue Consulting (www.metalogue.co.uk). In his work he is particularly interested in the role language, metaphor, story and narrative play in shaping, perpetuating, or changing the way we think about and act into organizations and other social groups. When not doing this you might also find him in a kayak. He lives with his wife and two children between Oxford, UK and Görlitz, Eastern Germany.

Photographs © Dirk Dobiéy 2017